The
Psychic
Sense

The
Psychic
Sense

How to Awaken Your
Sixth Sense to Solve Life's
Problems and Seize Opportunities

By Edgar Cayce

ARE
PRESS

ASSOCIATION FOR
RESEARCH AND
ENLIGHTENMENT

A.R.E. Press • Virginia Beach • Virginia

A.R.E. Press
215 67th Street
Virginia Beach, VA 23451-2061

Cayce, Edgar, 1877-1945.
The psychic sense : how to awaken your sixth sense to solve life's problems and seize opportunities / by Edgar Cayce
    p. cm.
ISBN 0-87604-523-9 (trade pbk.)
1. Psychic ability. 2. Parapsychology. I. Van Auken, John. II. Title.
BF1031.C475 2006
133.8—dc22

                        2006012855

Cover design by Richard Boyle

Contents

Foreword
Who Was Edgar Cayce?

"It is a time in the earth when people everywhere seek to know more of the mysteries of the mind, the soul," said my grandfather, Edgar Cayce, from an unconscious trance from which he demonstrated a remarkable gift for clairvoyance.

His words are prophetic even today, as more and more Americans in these unsettled times are turning to psychic explanations for daily events. For example, according to a survey by the National Opinion Research Council nearly half of American adults believe they have been in contact with someone who has died, a figure twice that of ten years earlier. Two-thirds of all adults say they have had an ESP experience; ten years before that figure was only one-half.

Every culture throughout history has made note of its own members' gifted powers beyond the five senses. These rare individuals held special interest because they seemed able to provide solutions to life's pressing problems. America in the twenty-first century is no exception.

Edgar Cayce was perhaps the most famous and most carefully documented psychic of our time. He began to use his unusual abilities when he was a young man, and from then on for over forty years he would, usually twice a day, lie on a couch, go into a sleeplike state, and respond to questions. Over fourteen thousand of these discourses, called readings, were carefully transcribed by his secretary and preserved by the Edgar Cayce Foundation in Virginia Beach, Virginia. These psychic readings continue to provide inspiration, insight, and help with healing to tens of thousands of people.

Having only an eighth–grade education, Edgar Cayce lived a plain and simple life by the world's standards. As early as his childhood in Hopkinsville, Kentucky, however, he sensed that he had psychic ability. While alone one day he had a vision of a woman who told him he would have unusual power to help people. He also related experiences of "seeing" dead relatives. Once, while struggling with school lessons, he slept on his spelling book and awakened knowing the entire contents of the book.

As a young man he experimented with hypnosis to treat a recurring throat problem that caused him to lose his speech. He discovered that under hypnosis he could diagnose and describe treatments for the physical ailments of others, often without knowing or seeing the person with the ailment. People began to ask him other sorts of questions, and he found himself able to answer these as well.

In 1910 the *New York Times* published a two–page story with pictures about Edgar Cayce's psychic ability as described by a young physician, Wesley Ketchum, to a clinical research society in Boston. From that time on people from all over the country with every conceivable question sought his help.

In addition to his unusual talents, Cayce was a deeply religious man who taught Sunday school all of his adult life and read the entire Bible once for every year that he lived. He always tried to attune himself to God's will by studying the Scriptures and maintaining a rich prayer life, as well as by trying to be of service to those who came seeking help. He used his talents only for helpful purposes. Cayce's simplicity and humility and his commitment to doing good in the world continue to attract people to the story of his life and work and to the far-reaching information he gave.

Charles Thomas Cayce, Ph.D.
Executive Director
Association for Research and Enlightenment, Inc.

Editor's Explanation of Cayce's Discourses

Edgar Cayce dictated all of his discourses from a self-induced trance. A stenographer took his discourses down in shorthand and later typed them. Copies were sent to the person or persons who had requested the psychic reading, and one was put into the files of the organization, which built up around Cayce over the years, the Association for Research and Enlightenment (better known as the A.R.E.).

In his normal consciousness, Edgar Cayce spoke with a Southern accent but in the same manner as any other American. However, from the trance state, he spoke in the manner of the King James Bible, using "thees" and "thous." In trance, his syntax was also unusual. He put phrases, clauses, and sentences together in a manner that slows down any reader and requires careful attention in order to be sure of his meaning. This caused his stenographer to adopt some unusual punctuation in order to put into sentence form some of the long, complex thoughts conveyed by Cayce while in trance. Also, many of his discourses are so jam-packed with information and insights that it requires that one slow down and read more carefully in order to fully understand what he is intending.

From his trance state, Cayce explained that he got his information from two sources: (1) the inquiring individual's mind, mostly from his or her deeper, subconscious mind and (2) from the Universal Consciousness, the infinite mind within which the entire universe is conscious. He explained that every action and thought of every individual makes an impression upon the Universal Consciousness, an impression that can be psychically read. He correlated this with the Hindu concept of an Akashic Record, which is an ethereal, fourth–dimensional film upon which actions and thoughts are recorded and can be read at any time.

When giving one of his famous health readings, called physical readings, Cayce acted as if he were actually scanning the entire body of the person, from the inside out! He explained that the subconscious mind of everyone contains all of the data on the condition of the physical body it inhabits, and Cayce simply connected with the patient's deeper mind. He could also give the cause of the condition, even if it was from early childhood or from many lifetimes ago in a previous incarnation of the soul. This was knowable because the soul remembers all of its experiences. He explained that deeper portions of the subconscious mind are the mind of the soul, and portions of the subconscious and the soul are in the body with the personality.

In life readings and topic readings, Cayce also connected with the subconscious minds of those inquiring as well as the Universal Consciousness.

Occasionally, Cayce would not have the material being requested, and he would say, "We do not have that here." This implied that Cayce's mind was more directed than one might think. He was not open to everything. From trance, he explained that the suggestion given at the beginning of one of his psychic readings so directed his deeper mind and focused it on the task or subject requested that he truly did not have other topics available. However, on a few occasions, he seemed able to shift topics in the middle of a reading.

The typed readings have a standard format. Numbers were used in the place of the name of the person or persons receiving the reading, and a dash system kept track of how many readings the person had received. For example, reading 137-5 was the fifth reading for Mr. [137]. At the top of the reading are the reading number, the date and location, and the names or numbers (for privacy) of those in attendance. Occasionally the stenographer would include a note about other conditions, such as the presence of a manuscript that the in–trance Cayce was supposed to view psychically and comment on. In many cases, I left in the entire format of a recorded reading, but sometimes only a paragraph or two were pertinent to our study, and then I only give the reading number. As I explained, Cayce dictated all of these discourses while he was in trance. In most cases, he spoke in a monotone voice. However, he would sometimes elevate his volume when saying a word or phrase. In these instances, his stenographer usually typed these words with all-capital letters, to give the reader some sense of Cayce's increased volume. These all-capital letters have been changed to italic typeface for readability, as well as emphasis. In many cases, these words appear to be rightly accentuated in Cayce's discourses. However, in some cases, it is not clear why he raised his voice.

Another style that the stenographer adopted was to capitalize all of the letters in Cayce's many affirmations (positive-thought or prayer-like passages to be used by the recipient as a tool for focusing and/or raising consciousness). I have also changed these to upper- and lower-case letters and italicized them. Questions asked Cayce have also been italicized for easier reference.

Whenever his stenographer was not sure if she had written down the correct word or thought that she might have missed or misunderstood a word, she inserted suggested words, comments, and explanations in [brackets]. If she knew of another reading that had similar material or that was being referred to during this reading, she would put the reading number in brackets. Cayce's entire collection of readings is available on CD-ROM from the A.R.E., so, even though the referenced reading may not be in this book, I left these references in for any future research; but several of the readings that have references are in this book. Within the text of a reading, all (parentheses) are asides made by Cayce himself while in trance, not by his stenographer. She only used [brackets] within the text of a reading. In the preliminary material, she used parentheses in the normal manner. My comments are indicated by the term "Editor's Note."

A few common abbreviations use in these discourses were: "GD" for Gladys Davis, the primary stenographer; "GC" for Gertrude Cayce, Edgar's wife and the predominant conductor of the readings, and "EC" for Edgar Cayce.

—John Van Auken, Editor

1

●

Cayce's Initial Series on the Psychic Sense

Text of Reading 3744-1

This Psychic Reading given by Edgar Cayce at the Phillips
Hotel, Dayton, Ohio, this 18th day of June, 1923.

PRESENT

Edgar Cayce; Arthur Lammers (?), Conductor; Fay Autry,
Steno. Linden Shroyer.

READING

Time of Reading Unknown.

(Q) What is the state of the physical forces of this body while giving this work?

(A) They, the physical are under subjugation of the subconscious or
soul forces. As we see in the body we have the Trinity for an entity. We
have as this:

The physical forces and mental mind; we have the spirit or soul force
with the superconscience [superconscious?] or soul mind; then we have the
spirit, that is, the mind of the soul force, just as the soul occupies the
body in its same form and manner. Just so as the body of an individual
that has past [passed?] beyond may be seen by others in the physical plane
only when their physical or mental, material or mental are subjugated.

When this body here, we are speaking of, Edgar Cayce, the physical is subjugated or laid aside, we find the soul forces give the information, and the body is under the subjugation of the soul and spirit forces.

(Q) Mr. Cayce, what is the soul of a body?

(A) That which the Maker gave to every entity or individual in the beginning, and which is seeking the home again or place of the Maker.

(Q) Does the soul ever die?

(A) May be banished from the Maker, not death.

(Q) What is the subconscience [subconscious?] mind of the body?

(A) An attribute of the soul.

(Q) What position should this body get in when going into this state?

(A) There is no stated position. The body may as well be in one position as another. In whatever position that it becomes easier for a body or this body, Edgar Cayce, we are to be able to put the physical under subjugation, that position assume or take.

(Q) Why do the arms ache after the body comes out of this state and back to normal?

(A) The last of the body re-entering as in the beginning of the personel [personality?]. The body gives off the radiation and it reaches the arms, for they are as in contraction, as might be given from heat to metal that governs and becomes the first and the last to receive and give off that radiated.

(Q) Is there any way to overcome this?

(A) Should not be wanted to be overcome. Rather the knowledge that the force is in perfect accord with forces when resistance or when imperfect accord is made or when suggestions are causing the deflection of truth. We do not have the actions when in normal or physical, material normal.

(Q) Give word for word what should be used to take a reading properly and to secure the best results, that is, to cause this body to go into this state, while he is in this state, and how to bring him out of this state and back to normal?

(A) The body is only perfect normal while in this state. Those on the physical plane should first know that, that which will reach the nearer accord or harmony between the individuals through which the information is attempted to be obtained, that is, the correct manner, as we have here with this individual and entity. The correct, and this case would be word for word as this: "Now the body is assuming its normal forces and will be able and will give such information as is desired of it at the present time. The body, physically, will be perfectly normal and will give that information now," then the name, the suggestion of what is desired, and the minds must be in perfect accord without the vibrations being apart [abnormal?]. When the information is obtained, the body would then say: "Now the body will be so equalized as to overcome all those things that might hinder or prevent from being and giving its best mental, spiritual and physical self. Now perfectly normal and balanced, wake up."

(Q) *Should the body wake up immediately or wait a minute and a half or so?*

(A) Just as we have given. When the conditions assumed this position the body of itself is normal to be awake whether it be moments or weeks or minutes.

(Q) *When is the correct time to say what you have given?*

(A) As the body assumes or passes into this presence here or this state as here.

(Q) *What kind of questions should be asked?*

(A) Only those that are in accord with spiritual and soul forces and laws, which are as these: That which is willing to assist or to make the All better, and by better we mean, relief from pain, suffering of any kind or character without the expense of another individual.

(Q) *Should all questions be positive or negative?*

(A) Positive. Negative gives deflection.

(Q) *Is the information always absolutely correct?*

(A) In so far as it is in accord with the soul forces or matter, and so long as the information desiring to be obtained is in that channel or so long as there is harmony between the one and the other, just as we have given, reflection so far as the deflection is made by the individual through their own suggestion guides or directs the information as it comes to the physical plane. The soul or subconscience [subconscious?] self of this body, Edgar Cayce, is in the state of being guided by the individual who makes the suggestions, and so long as the suggestions are in accord and the mind of the individual is kept in accord, correct—shaded just that much.

(Q) *Is it best that one person take the readings or more than one?*

(A) Only one can make them correctly.
(Q) Should there be a variety of persons making the suggestions?
(A) Only one person may. Deflections come more when individual is governed or turned aside by others. There may be at different times more than one. In the making of an individual, as we find the body here on the physical plane, the entity meaning the whole, you see, is made of both the opposite, or positive and negative poles. The body is not complete without the whole or both. We find this shown in the construction of man in many ways and is easily manifested to those who will only read the perfect union in all forces, whether of the physical, mental, material, soul or spirit, is when the two are combined in the body, hence in this individual personality and individuality, the negative often the truer, better information when in this condition. Find that individual.
(Q) In what manner can the person be chosen to take the readings to obtain the best results?
(A) It is given to the individual, whom obtains any vision of the super or soul plane to know when they are in accord with that individual. Sex as known on the material does not necessarily mean that a body is positive or negative, but only as shown from the soul or subconscience [subconscious?] or spiritual plane.
(Q) What kind of a person should make these suggestions?
(A) As we have given. Those whom are of the negative, for this entity or individual, Edgar Cayce, is the strong positive and must be reached through that channel, as we have given.
(Q) Is Fay Autry, who is in this room, alright to make these suggestions?
(A) Very good. Better than most of them.
(Q) What is the name of the person, who would be the best in the world to make these suggestions?
(A) Edwin Wroth.
(Q) Where is this body located at the present time?
(A) Severian, Bavaria.
(Q) Is he an American citizen?
(A) No.
(Q) What nationality is he?
(A) Russian.

(Q) When the case is such that a part or a certain point in a reading is not clear or lost to the person taking the reading why is it not possible to have repeated?

(A) When once past from the reflection as is shown in the first here, we find we have gone beyond that point or reflection and with the forcing of the condition we do not reach the point from which the reflection was first made.

(Q) Is the psychic phenomena an inherited trait?

(A) Not necessarily so unless the spirit or soul of the forces of those directly connected are transplanted in the one. The law of attraction is positive and remains with one. The material attraction is to be to those of the same form, as to whether the phenomena is produced by hereditary is far from being correct. Law of attraction would only draw. See, we have in this plane or sphere certain immutable laws. We have those that may be deflected by coming in contact with each other. The law that is unchangeable remains and is only deflected.

(Q) Can anyone else do this work besides Edgar Cayce?

(A) We have no work ahead of us.

(Q) Mr. Cayce, I mean the psychic phenonema [phenomenon?] or readings?

(A) All can do it.

(Q) How can this work be developed so that all can do it?

(A) All can already do it. As to the degree of the development, only the law of concentration through subjugation, as we have the law here, as this we illustrate conditions: Water occupies a certain place without changing of form. It always occupies that same place, though it is pliable. Air may be compressed without changing form, only needing the opportunities of the expression of its flexibility. One is no more flexible than the other, though air can occupy with water, same as we have with individuals in this sphere. With the subjugation of one of the elements or of the Trinity of the individual, those characters, those powers, those forces, those laws of the other portion of body are brought out into play and only need the opportunity of their self–expression.

(Q) Is this work harmful or detrimental to the physical and mental forces of this body?

(A) No. It may be abused as any force, either of the physical, mental, soul or spiritual force of the body. It may be made to become destructive by the misapplication, as we would have in just those elements as we have shown by the changing of form. Only a very thin veil between sublime and ridiculous, thinner between good and evil, whether applied to the physical, mental, soul or spiritual elements of the physical or material body as is manifested on this plane with its attributes. The highest attributes of the material body being what is called on this plane, the senses and the body is given the vehicle or mode of expressing the fundamentals or findings of its senses or psychic or soul force is expressed to the mental or physical plane through one of these senses, or made manifested thereby. The destructive forces may be made to govern or control any or all these senses in the physical. With the subjugation of one in the material we find some one or all of the others become highly attuned or more sensitive, the same as in the developing of those inclined by the forces, either of the laws being followed by attraction upon by material ability or forces as applied by the universal force in the attraction of other bodies or spheres governing the plane and under the force in which the body takes on sphere, its scope of living. In this manner the developing of the psychic or soul forces through one of the senses so governed may be developed to good or evil, as is classified in this sphere. Evil is only evil to him, who thinks it evil or to what sense it has become applied. All is good as used to the developing of any force under which its law applies.

(Q) *How should this work be used to be the most successful and to do the most good?*

(A) As has been applied and under the laws governing force as is shown in just what has been given to this individual body, Edgar Cayce, we are speaking of, as known on this plane, though this has covered eight generations. We have the forces as applied through that of the healing of physical ailments and that may border on to ailments of the soul and mental and spiritual forces.

(Q) *Is this work to be perpetuated?*

(A) That is its material force, its universal force, see.

(Q) *Is it time to start an institution for the carrying on of these readings?*

(A) Very good. The time is nigh, and not just as yet, not just as yet. Time does not mean anything. Those only be secular.

(Q) *Where should this hospital be?*

(A) Near the sea.

(Q) In the west or the east?

(A) Doesn't matter.

(Q) What is the significance of the dream, which has come to this body so often in past years, the dream of climbing a hill with a lady?

(A) All in this manifestation of forces from the universal force, only in symbolic forms. The two as shown represent the whole or entity that must exist for the better forces in the body, whether for secular or psychic, soul or spiritual reasons. None enter the presence of the Maker without its entity, hence the many laws and forces as shown in manifestated ways in the material world. The hill or descending only represents only as the living, way, with its pointing foliage as toward the heavens, almost up, only with secular ideas. The down road is followed, though strewn with the beauties of the universal forces in that covering the earth. The water or the living way as past with the beauty of all reacknowledged [?] [word was hand written] in the purity of the element itself. The messenger, the wavering of all the forces that secular element must enter in while this plane is being lead for the development of the soul forces. The mud and way representing that, the forces may be lead off from the better ways. The wall that is to be scaled being that which all must overcome, and that as the ones chosen to assist in mounting to the better ways do not lend their assistance they must be cut off, for we find as in this: Always the gold or that of the secular nature follows the other companion well in the one scaling to the top.

The body in this work gives of the forces as is made manifested to the elemental forces as vibrates through from the superconscience [superconscious?] or subconscience [subconscious?] or soul forces as by the touch, by suggestion, which produces the thought as given or made manifest in words.

(Q) Should the hospital be established in Dayton, Ohio?

(A) Be very good. There are others, as we have given, that are much better. There are elements and forces and the influence of those forces that must be considered for the best development of the work or of that expected and that may be accomplished through the work or made manifest to others. The better place would be Virginia or North or South Carolina. The influence from the forces as just given here, that the work as accomplished in Dayton would radiate out to produce those, that would bring about the establishing of the work, those forces that must be considered as to the better are the influences as are brought to bear on the life as lived by the individual itself, and those connected or associated with such work.

(Q) Just exactly what do you mean by this last statement?

(A) Just what it said. With a body surrounded with those elements that do not give the vibration that is in accord with the work attempting to be accomplished, there is not the best given off through the work itself. That element would develop itself in any place and especially in Dayton, Ohio.

(Q) Mr. Cayce, is it possible for Edgar Cayce to establish a hospital anywhere at present?

(A) Anywhere the body would see fit to establish it, it may be established.

(Q) Is it possible for the influences to be removed that cause it not to be best to establish a hospital here in Dayton, Ohio?

(A) We have just given that it is not best to be established in Dayton, Ohio. Why kick against the pricks? (Virginia Beach)

(Q) Should the hospital be established near Virginia Beach?

(A) Very good.

(Q) In what spot in Virginia or North or South Carolina would it be best to establish the hospital?

(A) We have given it.

(Q) What should be the environment of this body when he is normal and when in this state?

(A) In the normal physical forces of this body, there should be the better forces and elements about this body, that which is in keeping with the work that is being attempted to be done—sufficient of the relaxing of the mental forces to keep the balance in the system. Remember that always that of the ordinary or not too strenuous forces of every character are the better elements with which to be surrounded— not prohibited of or licentious, but that of the mental or well balanced man or individual gives of the best under those conditions, whether in the plane of mental matter, physical matter, spiritual or soul or psychic forces. No one need to be expected to obtain the best under strain or by pressure. Only elemental forces are changed by too much pressure or too lax conditions.

(Q) *How should the body govern his regularity of meals?*

(A) Meet the needs as they present themselves.

(Q) *Should this body eat very much meats?*

(A) Not an excess of anything. Meats are not good for the body, only in moderation.

(Q) *How are the number of readings the body is able to give in any one day to be determined?*

(A) By the physical forces as manifested and by the conditions as they present themselves. An excess of any one thing or a laxness of any one thing is not good physically, spiritually, mentally, morally, financially or any other.

(Q) *Is the word "reading" proper for the usage of the information given?*

(A) Words mean nothing. Very good. Well as any other.

(Q) *In what manner of explanation may this work be presented to other people so that they may understand it clearly?*

(A) Any manner or form of work of any nature only given credence by the results obtained. With the results all are interested in, present those.

(Q) *Does the information given through these readings come from the subjective to the objective mind?*

(A) We have just given it.

(Q) *Mr. Cayce, will you please tell me the difference between the subjective and objective mind?*

(A) One is an attribute of the physical, the other of the soul.

(Q) *Have the number of readings given in the last three weeks in Dayton been too much of a strain on the physical health of this body?*

(A) As we have given. The influence of any work depends upon the surrounding under which that is done. The work is not a physical strain on the body. It is the normal effect only. The strain comes between the subjective and objective forces within the body, and only by the right conducting of same can this body be protected from the unbalancing forces between the two. The fear to be is not of physical but of mental strain as known in the material world and forces. Those under which the body has been for the last three weeks has not been too many, for the whole physical force gains strength. Watch for the development in the mental when correctly and incorrectly conducted.

[Following is the second part of the discourse.]

Yes, we have the body here and these conditions. We have had this before, you see. The elemental forces in these we find show in their relativity to those that come in contract [contact?] with this at this time, and through those, the reflexes are given to the physical plane, as we have given here, you see.

(Q) *What is the difference in suggestion to the subconscious mind and the conscious mind?*

(A) Suggestion to the conscious mind only brings to the mental plane, those forces that are of the same character and the conscious is the suggestion action. In that of suggestion to the subconscious mind gives its reflection or reaction from the universal forces or mind or superconscious forces.

(Q) *What is meant by ailments of the soul, mental and spiritual forces on which this work may border? [Note: this question was "crossed out" in the original manuscript and also appears below.]*

(A) By the suggestion just as given may be waved [waived?] by the forces that are brought to bear on the subconscious to reach the conscious mind, just as we have in a purely mechanical form. Any object or wood, especially, projected into water appears bended; just so with the reflection from suggestions to the subconscious to reach the conscious or mental forces appear bended in their action or in the manifestation of their action to the physical or conscious forces of individuals.

(Q) *Just what is meant by force and forces?*

(A) Depending upon the conditions under which incentive or that, which is being acted upon and that which is acting. As we have in the body of a living physical being, we have a body made up of many atoms, and their relation to each other depends upon the force as is given in each part to work upon or in or through the system. In the nerve system we find that of the force of physical matter or subconscious or soul matter, of superconscious or spirit matter, all receiving a force, as illustrated, we would have it here: When any object or injury comes to a portion of the body, then the nerves transmit that to the physical or conscious brain to be removed; the forces of all of the elementals or that is, of the parts of the body are brought into play; that which carries, that which replenishes, that which comes, that is force or forces, as may be. Or as we would have in the one word to express all force: That which is the spirit of any object, whether animate or inanimate, physical or material, that of the divine, which carries all force. We only have to take into consideration, but the relativity of the condition, position, time, place as to which or what element of force is implied in giving the elements of force from the subconscious force to the conscious force. In this also we may see how the correct reflection may appear bended.

(Q) *Is it possible for this body, Edgar Cayce, in this state to communicate with anyone who has passed into the spirit world?*

(A) The spirit of all that have passed from the physical plane remain about the plane until their development carry them onward or are returned for their development here. When they are in the plane of communication or remain within this sphere, any may be communicated with. There are thousands about us here at present.

(Q) *In the subconscious giving this information when in this state, how are we to know on the physical plane from whence and from which condition it gives this information?*

(A) Just as we know as to the force implied from whatever element the force is given, we must know from that force the information is obtained, deflected only by the expression of the individual, whom obtains the information, by the results obtained in the end. Just as we have in the diagnosis is for the betterment or advancement of the individual, just as the subconscious that communicates to the physical for with the physical submerged, a universal condition. It may be obtained from all or in part, just as needs for the individual. None is gained from one individual, but as there are good personages, there are good individuals, not necessarily within the same manifested body—just so in the spirit force there are good and there are bad personages still reflected. As these give rise to the expression and all give expression of experience of themselves of the entity through which the information is obtained gives that deflection as we may find with the surroundings of those not good, we will find the results in the same. Results in diagnosis give of the forces whether from the spirit forces are good or material forces are good, then judge. Just as the seed of truth is ever the same, and its productions are ever by the same, though some may fall in fallow land or some may fall in stony land.

(Q) What is meant by the banishment of a soul? from its Maker?

(A) Of the will as given in the beginning to choose for self, as in the earthly plane, all insufficient matter is cast onto Saturn. To work out its own salvation as would be termed in the word, the entity or individual banishes itself or its soul, which is its entity.

(Q) What is meant by the re-entering of the personel [personality?] as in the beginning?

(A) The personel [personality?] is that as known on the physical plan when in the subconscious or when the subconscious controls, the personel [personality?] is removed from the individual, and only that of the other forces in the Trinity occupies the body and use only its elements to communicate as in this body here, as we have spoken of. With the submerging of the conscious to the subconscious or superconscious, the personel [personality?] of the body or earthly portions are removed and lie above the other body. They may be seen here, hence the distributing of those conditions brings distress to the other portions of the entity or individual. With the return then we find the personel [personality?] leaves those impressions with those portions of the body, as we have given for the arm force here, you see. [See reference to arms earlier in 3744-1.]

(Q) To what place or state does the subconscious pass to receive this information it gives?

(A) Just here in the same sphere as when the spirit or soul or spirit and soul are driven or removed from the body or person.

(Q) What is meant by negative questions giving deflection?

(A) With positive and negative, or as elements are as unchangeable laws, as we have given, as the creator or the first cause is all positive that which is made negative.

(Q) What determines whether a body be positive or negative?

(A) Just as we have given, is it of a creative force, or it the creative force? Is it the force producing or, is it that produced? Just as we have in sex force known on this plane: Man, the producer, woman, that produced. One positive, the other negative. That is the law.

(Q) Why is Fay Autry, who is now in this room, better than most people to make

these suggestions to Edgar Cayce, while he is in this state?
(A) She is negative.
(Q) How is the name spelled, of the best person in the world to make these suggestions?
(A) E–d–w–i–n R–o–t–h.
(Q) Why is he the best person in the world to make these suggestions.
(A) Negative.
(Q) What is his business or profession?
(A) Scientist is his first appearance on this plane as a man.
(Q) Is he a medical man?
(A) He has been. Not at present. We are through.
(Q) Spell the name of the town, state and country in which he is located at present?
(A) Serben Servia Bavaria.
(Q) In what manner can Edgar Cayce communicate with him?
(A) When the time has arrived, when these forces are to be made manifest to the populace, the forces will draw these bodies together, that the work may be shown in the manner that will be acceptable to all, who would seek the right way, as is shown through this work. This body must first enter into the holy of holies in the mount, before the time comes.
(Q) What is meant by aliments [ailments?] of the soul, mental and spiritual forces on which this work may border?
(A) Mental is of the physical, which with its relative forces connecting the soul force and unbalancing of the trugh [truth?] may perform on the soul forces that which brings abnormal results to physical and soul matter. The correction of these only means that it, the work, assists the individual or the entity to find itself and to follow in that way that would lead that individual to its own better self. Each individual must leads its own life, whether in this sphere or in the other planes. The environment makes or performs the variations in whatever it may enter, else we would have no redemption in the blood.
(Q) How can this body go about the establishing of a hospital at any place at the present time?
(A) Only has to choose where that this institution or hospital is to be located, and then call on the forces to direct the manner and means of the physical show or building of such a place.

(Q) Does the environment have any bearing on the results obtained when the body is in this state?

(A) Environment bends the weakest and the strongest not in the same means, but we have given the environment carried on to the re–entering of the entity.

(Q) Is it a strain on the person, who makes the suggestions or conducts the readings, either mentally or physically?

(A) When properly done, no. Each individual has its own set laws of strain on physical or mental forces. With the conducting of the universal force or law, one correctly dividing should gain strength. If not balanced correctly, they may make it a detriment to their physical or mental force. It is their own making, just given strength. Just as the physical of the body, the more often it enters the presence of the universal force, gains strength, that is, when done in moderation. Moderation is as we have given. The pivot, as it were, of all force, strength or weakness, high or low, no excess in any direction good for any force.

(Q) Why are there times when the forces say "We are through", when they haven't completed the work attempting to be done?

(A) Being deflected to, to force an extent by question or environment as to cause the distress to the connection between the conscious and the subconscious or superconscious forces. A digression of the law forces the issue before it becomes a transgression of the law. Law is love, love is law.

(Q) What persons now in Dayton, Ohio should be associated with Edgar Cayce in this work?

(A) These will not be given from this plane.

(Q) Why do the forces sometime answer questions after they say they are through?

(A) Suggestion by the director or by environment from those present have again entered within the law, as we haven [have given?]. That makes the digression.

(Q) Why can one individual get a better reading than another?

(A) For the same reason as we have given of how it becomes a hardship on an individual to be or act as director. The one nearer in accord or keeping the negative force that the positive question may be given to the forces keep or give the better force . . . [Editor's Note: To stay on point, a paragraph has been removed.]

(Q) Is memory thought, or thought memory?

(A) With the evolving of the individual, the thought becomes a part of the memory as evolved through the developing of the entity. In memory, we may have from either plane, in physical or mental speaking—they are separate. In that of spirit and soul forces, thought and memory are as the entity. If not with spirit, thought and memory depending then upon the plane from which the question is approached. Physically, memory and thought are not synonymous, neither are they of the same beginning in physical forces. In that of the soul and spirit force, they become one and the same in evolution.

(Q) In the physical plane, do the thoughts of a person of another affect the other person either mentally or physically?

(A) Depending upon the development of the individual to whom the thought may be directed. The possibilities of the developing of thought transference is first being shown, evolution, you see. The individuals from this plane will and are developing this as the senses were and are developed.

Text of Reading 3744-2

This psychic reading given by Edgar Cayce at the Phillips Hotel, Dayton, Ohio, this 8th day of October, 1923, in accordance with request made by [5717], [953], [294], [4121] and [5453].

PRESENT

Edgar Cayce; Linden Shroyer, Conductor; Mamie Rosenberg, Steno. Others (?).

READING

Time of Reading, Phillips Hotel, 3:00 P.M. Dayton, Ohio.

(Q) Please give a definition of psychic phenomena.

(A) *Psychic* means of the *spirit* or *soul,* for cooperation of the Phenomena, or manifestation of the workings of those forces within the individual, or through the individual, from whom such phenomena, or of such phases of the working of the spirit and soul, to bring the actions of these to the physical plane, Phenomena meaning only the act itself, brought to the attention, or manifested in such a way as to bring the attention of an individual to the work itself. [See 900-19 for expansion on this.]

Psychic in the broader sense meaning spirit, soul, or the imagination of the mind, when attuned to the various phases of either of these two portions of the entity of an individual, or from the entity of others who are passed into the other planes than the physical or material; yet in the broader sense, the phenomena of psychic forces is as material as the forces that become visible to the material or physical plane. [See 900-19]

Psychic forces cover many various conditions, depending upon the development of the individual, or how far distant the entity is from the plane of spirit and soul forces.

Psychic means not understood from the physical, or material, or conscious mind.

Psychic means that of the mind presenting the soul and the spirit entity as manifested in the individual mind. Then taking the phases of that force, we find all Psychic Phenomena or force, presented through one of the acknowledged five senses of the physical or material body—these being used as the mode of manifesting to individuals. Hence we would have in the truest sense, *psychic*, meaning the expression to the material world of the latent, or hidden sense of the soul and spirit forces, whether manifested from behind, or in and through the material plane.

(Q) *How many kinds of Psychic Phenomena are known to mankind at the present time?*

(A) Almost as many as there are individuals, each entity being a force, or world within itself. Those of the unseen forces become then the knowledge of the individual, the power of expression, or of giving the knowledge obtained, being of an individual matter.

(Q) *Definition of the word mind.*

(A) That which is the active force in an animate object; that is the spark, or image of the Maker. Mind is the factor that is in direct opposition of will. Mind being that control of, or being the spark of the Maker, the *will*, the individual when we reach the plane of man. Mind being and is the factor governing the contention, or the interlaying space, if you please, between the physical to the soul, and the soul to the spirit forces within the individual or animate forces. We have the manifestation of this within the lowest order of animal creation. These are developed as the mind is developed, both by the action of all of the senses of the body, as we have them developed in man. *Mind is that* that reasons the impressions from the senses, as they manifest before the individual.

The active principle that governs man. Mind a factor, as the senses are of the mind, and as the soul and spirit are factors of the entity, one in all, all in one. We are speaking from the normal plane, of course. As the impressions are reached to the storehouse of the body, the mind is that factor, that principle, that portion that either segregates, correlates or divides the impression to the portion needed, to develop the entity or physical force toward the spark or infinite force, giving the life force to the body. The mind may be classified into the two forces—that between the physical and soul, and that between the soul and spirit force. We see the manifestations of this, rather than the object or the mind itself. We find this always manifested through one of the senses, the same as we find the psychic forces a manifestation of the soul and spirit; the *mind* a manifestation of the physical.

With the division of the mind force as given, we see why in the physical plane individuals become misunderstood or misrepresented. They do not reach the same manifestations from other individuals. Hence the expression, "They are all of one mind." "To *do good*, they become of one mind, *to do evil* they are many." The nearer approach the mind comes to the divide, between the soul and spirit forces, the nearer we become to that infinite force that guides when it is allowed to the individual's actions day by day.

Definition of the words "conscious mind":

The *conscious* means *that* that is able to be manifested in the physical plane through one of the senses.

Definition of the word "sub-conscious mind":

That lying between the soul and spirit forces within the entity, and is reached more thoroughly when the conscious mind is under subjugation of the soul forces of the individual or physical body. We may see manifestation in those of the so-called spiritual minded people. The manifestation of the subconscious in their action. That portion of the body, better known as the one that propagates or takes care of the body —physical, mental, moral or what not, when it is not able to take care of itself.

Sub-conscious is unconscious force. This may be seen in every nerve end, in every muscular force. Subconscious action may be brought into manifestation by the continual doing of certain acts in the physical plane, so the body becomes unconscious of doing the acts that it does.

(Q) How can we best develop our sub-conscious minds to be of the most benefit to our fellow men while in the Physical plane of living?

(A) By developing the mental or physical mind toward the uplift of mankind toward the Maker, leaving those things behind that so easily beset the physical body. By the training of the mental, through physical force, the sub-conscious urge, as we have given, the faculty of doing in the right or direct way, and lending assistance to the uplift of all.

The *thought* held against an individual directs the mind either of masses or classes, whether toward good or bad.

Thought is reached through the physical forces, and by becoming a part of the physical or conscious mind either lends the strength of sub-conscious forces or allows the subconscious to direct. Not that the physical mind gives strength, but by allowing the sub-conscious to direct, and not building the barrier between to be overcome.

That to be overcome might as well be met in this plane, for it will have to be met before we can gain the entrance to the Holy of Holies. This is the manner in which to train or conduct the physical to lend the assistance to the subconscious forces to direct and give the help the world or populace needs.

(Q) Why do women usually show more interest in psychic matters than men do?

(A) For their minds, women, are filled, or left vacant for the study of spiritual forces more than men, for the same reason as we have given. What their minds fill or feed upon for development toward psychic forces comes from the subconscious or the spirit and soul minds.

(Q) Is it possible to give information through Psychic Readings that will lead to the cure of diseases now known as incurable?

(A) It is. That which *is* was produced from some force. Nothing is greater than the force producing it. *That* may be counteracted. The condition that exists in the physical bodies we find all produced by conditions that may be met. There are in truth no incurable conditions, though the condition may be changed, or the mode of the plane's existence changed. That which exists is and was produced from a first cause, and may be met or counteracted, or changed, for the condition is the breaking of a law, and the healing forces will of necessity become the compliance with other laws that meet the needs of the condition. The healing depends upon the individual, and the attitude taken toward conditions from all manner of ways, or of the perception or conscious-ness of force that may be manifested through the individual. As to the psychic forces, only can give that condition that is, or produced, and the compliance with the law that may make a given condition. The whole rests then with such an individual, and its conditions as is capable of being manifested through itself. Psychic Readings for conditions, as given, then may be of assistance in the understanding of the law to be met or complied with.

The evasion of a law only puts conditions off, and must eventually be met.

(Q) *Why do so many people ridicule the idea of good being obtained through Psychic Readings?*

(A) Lack of understanding of law governing so called psychic force, or powers.

The lack of understanding is lack of consciousness being brought to the individual of potential powers that are manifest in and through psychic or occult forces. Many are caused by the lack of the proper usage of the knowledge or understanding obtained through such force, for the incorrect use of such knowledge may and would bring destruc-tive elements.

The lack then of discernment between that which is of physical, physical—material, material—and that of soul and spirit, which is in reality the life giving force in any object. The only real life being that which in the material or physical plane is called psychic. The ridicule then being only that of mis-application or mis-understanding or mis-use of the condition that is to be met, and that with which it is to be met.

Ridicule of such forces rather than being condemned, those are to be pitied, for they must eventually reach that condition where the soul awakens to the elements that are necessary for the developing, for with-out the psychic force in the world the physical would be in that condi-tion of "hit or miss", or that as a ship without a rudder or pilot, for that

element that is the building force in each and every condition is the
spirit or soul of that condition which is the psychic or occult force. No
healing is perfected without some psychic force exerted. For, as we
would have, whether of operative or of medicinal forces, or of directing
of organic forces to produce within themselves, that necessary to com-
pete with conditions found within the body in distress or disease. The
force represented, that counteracts, is nothing more or less than the
active force exerted in psychic force, as has been outlined in which is
psychic force. All of the elements that go to make up the expressions
reached to the mental forces of an individual, are actions of the psychic
forces from another individual, and is the collaboration of truth as
found in the individual or entity expressing, or manifesting itself, one
with the other. [See 900–25] Hence, the force in the violation of law of
curative forces, for mental or physical conditions existing within the
man.

(Q) *What period in the world's history were Psychic Readings given?*

(A) That as given among the Chaldeans was first used as the means of
assistance to the physical bodies. Not as applied in the present day
usage of such force or Phenomena, but that as the natural means of
expression of that unseen force of the soul and spirit of an earthly individual manifesting with and through the material or physical body, and
giving that life giving flow of such manifestations, nearly four thousand
years before the Prince of Peace came.

(Q) *Should Psychic Readings be used for purposes other than for the assistance of
curing human ills?*

(A) That knowledge of all universal force that may be obtained
through the psychic force is that of man's individual condition to be
dealt with. All force that may be obtained from such source, and not
used as self-aggrandizement, or for the selfish purposes of the physical
attributes, may be, should be, used and given to the world.

The understanding of all laws, for that is the law, the understanding
of the law pertaining to any given condition. Then we would give any
condition that may be met through such knowledge without the advantage taken of another individual, through its lack of such law or
knowledge should be used. The use of psychic force by any individual,
is only the using of that spiritual law that makes one free, but not free-

dom to take advantage, no more than that the gods [See 3744-5 re gods] take advantage of the knowledge of man's weaknesses to use them as means of destructive forces.

Through man, all law to the physical plane or material plane is made manifest, but the manifestation is of the compliance as made with the law. The knowledge of such gained through psychic force cannot be abused without receiving the same condition under which this puts such a condition upon the individual.

(Q) Give a clear definition of the word faith with reference to faith as required by one who is sick and desirous of being helped through Psychic Readings.

(A) In what faith means to the individual, as we have faith in the substance, or that which is hoped for, with the evidences from things seen or of things unseen. As in this, the desire of the heart or issues of life to be the assistance not from self, but even as the Maker gives, as is given that love is law. Law is love. Love is giving. Giving is as God, the Maker.

Text of Reading 3744-3

This psychic reading given by Edgar Cayce, at the Phillips Hotel, Dayton, Ohio, this 9th day of October, 1923, in accordance with request made by [5717], [294], and others.

PRESENT

Edgar Cayce; Linden Shroyer, Conductor; Mamie Rosenberg, Steno.

READING

Time of Reading, Phillips Hotel, 11:00 A.M., Dayton, Ohio.

(Q) From what source does this body EC derive its information? [See same question answered also in 294-1 (year 1910?).]

(A) The information as given or obtained from this body is gathered from the sources from which the suggestion may derive its information.

In this state the conscious mind becomes subjugated to the subconscious, superconscious or soul mind; and may and does communicate with like minds, and the subconscious or soul force becomes universal.

From any subconscious mind information may be obtained, either from this plane or from the impressions as left by the individuals that have gone on before, as we see a mirror reflecting direct that which is before it. It is not the object itself, but that reflected, as in this: The suggestion that reaches through to the subconscious or soul, in this state, gathers information from that as reflected from what has been or is called real or material, whether of the material body or of the physical forces, and just as the mirror may be waved or bended to reflect in an obtuse manner, so that suggestion to the soul forces may bend the reflection of that given; yet within, the image itself is what is reflected and not that of some other.

Through the forces of the soul, through the mind of others as presented, or that have gone on before; through the subjugation of the physical forces in this manner, the body obtains the information.

(Q) *In obtaining this information by suggestion, does this body gain this information from the director or from the body directed to?*

(A) From the subconscious forces, which become universal by the natural laws governing *relativity of all force*: whether spirit, soul or physical, and the information is obtained through that connection between subconscious soul or spirit forces as directed, and directed to. Suggestion being that manner in which the direction is given. Hence, how the reflections, either direct or wavered, are obtained, just as the subconscious force of the director is held in that

direction the information is obtained and in the manner that it, the director's subconscious wavers, the reflections becomes in the same manner wavered.

(Q) *In giving diagnosis of the physical body, how are internal conditions reflected?*

(A) By relativity of force.

(Q) *What is the state of the physical forces of this body while giving this work?*

(A) They, the physical, are under subjugation of the subconscious or soul forces. As we see in the body we have the trinity for an entity. We have as this: the physical forces and mental mind; we have the spirit or soul force with the superconscious or soul mind; then we have the spirit that is the mind of the soul force, just as the soul occupies the body in its same form and manner. Just as the body of an individual that has passed beyond may be seen by others in the physical plane only when their physical or mental, material or mental are subjugated like this body here we are speaking of, Edgar Cayce, the physical is subjugated or laid aside, we find the soul forces give the information, and the body is under the subjugation of the soul and spirit forces.

(Q) *What is the soul of a body?*

(A) That which the Maker gave to every entity or individual in the beginning, and which is seeking the home or place of the Maker.

(Q) *Does the soul ever die?*

(A) May be banished from the Maker, not death.

(Q) *What is the subconscious mind of the body?*

(A) An attribute of the soul or mind of the soul.

(Q) *What is the difference in suggestion to the subconscious mind and the conscious mind?*

(A) Suggestion to the conscious mind only brings to the mental plane those forces that are of the same character and the conscious is the suggestion in action. In that of suggestion to the subconscious mind, it gives its reflection or reaction from the universal forces or mind or superconscious forces. By the suggestion just as given may be wavered by the forces that are brought to bear on the subconscious to reach the conscious mind, just as we have in a purely mechanical form. [See 900-59] Any object, or wood especially, projected into water, appears bent; just so with the reflection from suggestions to the subconscious to reach the conscious or mental forces appear bent in their action, or in the manifestation of their action, to the physical or conscious forces of individuals.

(Q) *Just what is meant by force and forces?*

(A) Depending upon the conditions under which incentive or that which is being acted upon and that which is acting.

As we have in the body of a living physical being, we have a body made up of many atoms, and their relations to each other depends upon the force as is given in each part to work upon, or in or through the system.

In the nerve system we find that of the force of physical matter or subconscious or soul matter, or superconscious or spirit matter, all receiving a force, as illustrated, we would have it here; when any object or injury comes to a portion of the body, then the nerves transmit that to the physical or conscious brain to be removed; the forces of all of the elements or, that is, of the parts of the body are brought into play. That which carries, that which replenishes, that which comes, such force or forces, as may be. Or as we would have in the one word to express all force; that which is the spirit of any object [See 900–59], whether animate or inanimate, physical or material, that of the Divine which carries all force. We only have to take into consideration the relativity of the condition, position, time and place as to which or what element of force is implied in giving the elements of force from the subconscious force to the conscious force. In this also we may see how the correct reflections may appear bent.

(Q) Is it possible for this body, Edgar Cayce, in this state, to communicate with anyone who has passed into the spirit world?

(A) The spirit of all that have passed from the physical plane remain about the plane until their development carry them onward or are returned for their development here, when they are in the plane of communication or remain within this sphere, any may be communicated with. There are thousands about us here at present.

(Q) If the subconscious is giving this information when in this state, how are we to know on the physical plane from whence and from which condition it gives this information?

(A) Just as we know as to the force implied from whatever element the force is given, we must know from that force the information is obtained, deflected only by the expression of the individual who obtains the information. By the results obtained in the end. Just as we have in the diagnosis is for the betterment or advancement of the individual, just as the subconscious that communicates to the physical, for with the physical submerged, a universal condition. It may be obtained from all or in part, just as needs for the individual. None is gained from one individual, but as there are good personages, there are good individuals, not necessarily within the same manifested body—just so in spirit force there are good and there are bad personages still reflected. As those give rise to the expression and all give expression of experience of themselves of the entity through which the information is obtained gives that deflection as we may find with the surroundings of those not good, we will find the results in the same. Results in diagnosis give of the forces, whether the spirit forces are good or material forces are good. Then judge. Judge as the seed of truth is ever the same, and its production are ever by the same, though some may fall in fallow land or some may fall in stony land.

(Q) *What is meant by banishment of a soul from its Maker?*

(A) Of the will as given in the beginning to choose for self as in the earthly plane, all insufficient matter is cast unto Saturn. To work out his own salvation as would be termed in the word, the entity or individual banishes itself, or its soul, which is its entity.

(Q) *What is meant by the re-entering of the personality as in the beginning?*

(A) The personality is that as known on the physical plane in the subconscious or when the subconscious controls, the personality is removed from the individual, and only that other forces in the trinity occupying the body and using only its elements to communicate as in this body here, we have spoken of. With the submerging of the conscious to the subconscious, the personality of the body or earthly portions are removed and lie above the other body. They may be seen here. Hence the disturbing of those conditions bring distress to the other portions of the entity or individual. With the return then we find the personality leaves those impressions with those portions of the body, as we have given for the arm force here, you see.

(Q) To what place or state does the subconscious pass to receive this information it gives?

(A) Just here in the same sphere as when the spirit or soul or spirit and soul are driven or removed from the body or persons.

(Q) *What is meant by ailment of the soul, mental and spiritual forces on which this work may border?*

(A) Mental is of the physical which with its relative forces connecting the soul force and unbalancing of the truth may perform on the soul forces that which brings abnormal results to physical and soul matter. [See 900-59] The correction of these only means that it, the work, assists the individual or the entity to find itself and to follow in that way that would lead that individual to its own better self.

Each individual must lead his own life, whether in this sphere or in the other planes. The environment makes or performs the variations in whatever it may enter, else we would have no redemption in the blood.

(Q) Does the environment have any bearing on the results obtained when the body is in this state?

(A) Environment bends the weakest and the strongest. Not in the same means, but we have given the environment carried on to the re-entering of the entity.

(Q) Is memory thought, or thought memory?

(A) With the evolving of the individual, the thought becomes a part of the memory as evolved through the developing of the entity. In memory, we may have either plane, in physical or mental speaking—they are separate. In that of spirit and soul forces, thought and memory depending then upon the plane from which the question is approached. Physically, memory and thought are not synonymous, neither are they of the same beginning in physical forces. In that of the soul and spirit force, they become one and the same in evolution. [See 900-233]

(Q) In the physical plane, do the thoughts of another person affect a person either mentally or physically?

(A) Depending upon the development of the individual to whom the thought may be directed. The possibilities of the developing of thought transference is first being shown, evolution, you see. The individuals of this plane will and are developing this as the senses were and are developed.

Text of Reading 3744-4

This psychic reading given by Edgar Cayce at the Phillips Hotel, this 24th day of November, 1923, in accordance with request made by [5717], [953], [294], and others.

PRESENT

Edgar Cayce; Linden Shroyer, Conductor, Gladys Davis, Steno.

READING

Time of Reading, Phillips Hotel, 3:30 P.M., Dayton, Ohio.

(Q) Please give a definition of the word astrology.

(A) That position in space about our own earth that is under the control of the forces that are within the sphere of that control, and all other spheres without that control. That is astrology, the study of those conditions.

In the beginning, our own plane, the Earth, was set in motion. The planning of other planets began the ruling of the destiny of all matters as created, just as the division of waters was ruled and is ruled by the Moon in its path about the earth; just so as the higher creation as it begun is ruled by its action in conjunction with the planets about the earth. The strongest force used in the destiny of man is the Sun first, then the closer planets to the earth, or those that are coming to ascension at the time of the birth of the individual, *but let it be understood here, no action of any planet or the phases of the sun, the moon or any of the heavenly bodies surpass the rule of man's will power, the* power given by the Creator of man, in the beginning, when he became a living soul, with the power of choosing for himself. The inclinations of man are ruled by the planets under which he is born, for the destiny of man lies within the sphere or scope of the planets.

(Q) *Do the planets have an effect on the life of every individual born?*

(A) They have. Just as this earth's forces were set in motion, and about it, those forces that govern the elements, elementary so, of the earth's sphere or plane, and as each comes under the influence of those conditions, the influence is to the individual without regards to the will, which is the developing factor of man, in which such is expressed through the breath of the Creator, and as one's plane of existence is lived out from one sphere to another they come under the influence of those to which it passes from time to time.

In the sphere of many of the planets within the same solar system, we find they are banished to certain conditions in developing about the spheres from which they pass, and again and again and again return from one to another until they are prepared to meet the everlasting Creator of our entire Universe, of which our system is only a very small part. [See 900-25]

Be not dismayed [deceived]; God is not mocked; "Whatsoever a man soweth that shall he also reap." [Gal. 6:7]

In the various spheres, then, through which he must pass to attain that which will fit him for the conditions to enter in, and become a part of that Creator, just as an individual is a part of the creation now. In this manner we see there is the influence of the planets upon an individual, for all must come under that influence, though one may pass from one plane to another without going through all stages of the condition, for only upon the earth plane at present do we find man is flesh and blood, but upon others do we find those of his own making in the preparation of his own development.

As given, "The heavens declare the glory of God, and the firmament sheweth His handyworks. Day unto day uttereth speech, night unto night sheweth knowledge." This from the beginning and unto the end. [Ps. 19:1, 2]

Just in that manner is the way shown how man may escape from all of the fiery darts of the wicked one, for it is self, and selfishness, that would damn the individual soul unto one or the other of those forces that bring about the change that must be in those that willfully wrong his Maker. It is not that which man does or leaves undone, but rather that indifference toward the creation that makes or loses for the individual entity. Then, let's be up and doing—doing—"be ye doers [of the word], and not hearers only". [James 1:22]

(Q) *Give the names of the principal planets, and the influence on the lives of people.*

(A) Mercury, Mars, Jupiter, Venus, Saturn, Neptune, Uranus, Septimus. Influence as is given by many of those in and about the earth plane is defective. Many of the forces of each is felt more through the experience, by the entity's sojourn upon those planets than by the life that is lead other than by will, for will is the factor in the mind of man that must be exercised. The influence from any is from what planet that soul and spirit returns to bring the force to the earth individual, as it is breathed into the body, from whence did it come? that being the influence. Not the revolution of the ideas as given from those who study of those forces, but study those that come, as the Star of Bethlehem came to the earth as the individual pointing out the way to Truth, the Light, and others can only be such as prepare their way through that light and influence.

(Q) *Are any of the planets, other than the earth, inhabited by human beings or animal life of any kind?*

(A) No.

(Q) *Give the description of the planet nearest the earth at the present time, and its effect upon the people.*

(A) That planet now fast approaching the earth, under whose influence the earth's minds trend, will be for the next few years, as time is known here, is Mars, who will be only thirty-five million miles away from the earth in 1924. The influence will be felt as this recedes from the earth, and those of that nature; that is, given through sojourn there, express in their lives upon the earth the troublesome times that will arise, only being tempered with that of those who may be, and will be, coming from those of Jupiter, Venus and Uranus, those strong ennobling forces tempered by those of love and strength.

(Q) *What effect will the planet, Uranus, have on the people during the next two years?*

(A) We find in this planet those of the exceptional forces, those of the ultra forces, those that carry the extremes in every walk of physical life and forces, and these are those that will, in the next two years, especially, give of their strength to the greater force, as has been given. Those, tempered with the forces as received there, find in the tumultuous times that are to arise, the setting ready for their again forces. Well may the earth tremble under that influence in 1925 and 1927.

(Q) *Is it proper for us to study the effects of the planets on our lives in order to better understand our tendencies and inclinations, as influenced by the planets?*

(A) When studied aright, very, very, very much so. How aright then? In that influence as is seen in the influence of the knowledge already obtained by mortal man. Give more of that into the lives, giving the understanding *that the will must be the ever guiding factor to lead man on, ever upward.*

(Q) *In what way should astrology be used to help man live better in the present physical plane?*

(A) In that which the position of the planets give the tendencies in a given life, without reference to the will. Then let man, the individual, understand how *will* may overcome, for we all must overcome, if we would, in any wise, enter in. Not that the position gives man the transport, but that that force as manifested in the creation of man wherein choice between the good and evil, exercising highest will force, may be manifested the greater in man. *Do that.*

(Q) *Who were the first people in the world to use astrology, and what time in history was it first used?*

(A) Many, many thousands, thousands of years ago. The first record as is given is as that recorded in Job, who lived before Moses was.

(Q) Are the tendencies of an individual influenced most by the planets nearer the earth at the time of the individual's birth?

(A) At, or from that one whom is at the zenith when the individual is in its place or sphere, or as is seen from that sphere or plane the soul and spirit took its flight in coming to the earth plane. For each plane, in its relation to the other, is just outside, just outside, relativity of force, as we gather them together.

Text of Reading 3744-5

This psychic reading given by Edgar Cayce at the Phillips Hotel, Dayton, Ohio, this 14th day of February, 1924, in accordance with request made by [5717], [953], [294], and others.

PRESENT

Edgar Cayce; Linden Shroyer, Conductor; Gladys Davis, Steno.

READING

Time of Reading Phillips Hotel, 3:00 P.M. Dayton, Ohio.

(Q) What are the laws governing relativity of all force?

(A) In giving the manifestation of such an law, which does exist, we first must consider that, that is called force, and that force then in its relation, or the relativity of that force to all force.

There are, as were set in the beginning, as far as the concern is of this physical earth plane, those rules or laws in the relative force of those that govern the earth, and the beings of the earth plane, and also that same law governs the planets, stars, constellations, groups, that that constitutes the sphere, the space, in which the planet moves. These are of the one force, and we see the manifestation of the relation of one force with another in the many various phases as is shown, for in fact that which to the human mind exists, in fact does not exist, for it has been in past before it is to the human mind in existence.

In this, we see the law of the relations of conditions, space or time and its relation to human mind, as is capable of obtaining information upon the earth plane from a normal force or conditions. Hence, we bring the same word, relativity of force, to prove its own self, and condition, for we have as in this:

The earth in its motion, held in space by that force of attraction, or detraction, or gravitation, or lack of gravitation in its force, so those things that do appear to have reality, and their reality to the human mind, have in reality passed into past conditions before they have reached the mind, for with the earth's laws, and its relations to other spheres, has to man become a past condition. So it is reached only in the further forces as will show, and as is given, for man to understand in this developing, or this evolution from sphere to sphere, or from plane to plane, in this condition.

Hence, we find to the normal mind, there is no law as to relativity of force, save as the individual may apply same in the individual's needs of them. That is sufficient.

(Q) What is meant by the Gods of the Universe referred to in the readings? [See 3744-2]

(A) Just as in this. All force has its incentive, the directing or creating of that force. That force to the human mind apparent, as different conditions, or relations, as referred to as the God, or the ruling force, of that individual force, as is giving the expression, and is referred to as the God, as of War, as of Peace, as of Water, as of the elements under the Sea. As of those above, as the God of High Heaven, the ruler over all, the one in all and the all in one.

(Q) Give the best method of helping the human family increase in knowledge of the subconscious soul or spirit world.

(A) The knowledge of the subconscious of an entity, or an individual, in or of the human family, is as of one integral force, or element, or self in the creation of the human family, and until the entity, or individual, as individuals, make this known to groups, classes, countries, nations, the greater study of self, that force will only be magnified. That of the spirit is the spark, or portion of the Divine that is in every entity, whether complete or of the evolution to that completeness.

The study from the human standpoint, of subconscious, subliminal, psychic, soul forces, is and should be the great study for the human family, for through self man will understand its Maker when it understands its relation to its Maker, and it will only understand that through itself, and that understanding is the knowledge as is given here in this state.

Each and every person getting that understanding has its individual force toward the great creation, and its individual niche, place or unit to perform. Has to reach numbers of psychic forces or phenomena that may be manifested in the earth plane, all the same, yet the understanding for the individual entity, viewed from its own standpoint, with its knowledge, is obtained and made ready by itself, to be manifested through itself, towards its own development, and in that development of the creation or world. In this manner, and in this form, and in this way, will the development (*to study the force as given through this manner*) be of assistance to the world.

As in dreams, those forces of the subconscious, when taken or correlated into those forms that relate to the various phases of the individual, give to that individual the better understanding of self, when correctly interpreted, or when correctly answered.

Forget not that it has been said correctly that the Creator, the Gods and the God of the Universe, speak to man through this individual self. Man approaches the nearer condition of its approach to that field when the normal is at rest; sleep or slumber, and when more of the forces are taken into consideration, and are studied by the individual (not someone else) it is the individual's job, each individual's condition, each individual's position, each individual's relation, each individual's manifestation, each individual's receiving the message from the higher forces themselves, and for each individual to understand if they will study, to show themselves approved.

"In all thy getting, my son, get understanding." [Prov. 4:7] That of Self. When one understands self, and self's relation to its Maker, the duty to its neighbor, its own duty to self, it cannot, it will not be false to man, or to its Maker. Give then more thought, *for thoughts are deeds*, and are children of the relation reached between the mental and the soul, and has its relation to spirit and soul's plane of existence, as they do in the physical or earth plane. What one thinks continually, they become; what one cherishes in their heart and mind they make a part of the pulsation of their heart, through their own blood cells, and build in their own physical, that which its spirit and soul must feed upon, and that with which it will be possessed, when it passes into the realm for which the other experiences of what it has gained here in the physical plane, must be used.

The attributes of the soul and spirit are as many, and as many more, as the attributes of the physical or mental mind. Each, in the beginning, endowed with that same condition—position. Each, in itself, building to itself, through its development known through the ages, as called from the earth plane, that which is manifest upon the earth. With each development, that force, known upon the plane as *will*, is given to man over and above all creation; *that* force that may separate itself from its Maker, for with the *will* man may either adhere or contradict the Divine law— those immutable laws, as are set between the Creator and the created.

The study of these, through their phases and forms, and especially through any of those phases, wherein the carnal or material or normal forces are laid aside, and the ever present elements of spirit and soul commune with those of the forces as found in each entity. Study those and *know thyself.*

(Q) *What is the law of love?*

(A) Giving. As is given in this injunction, "Love Thy Neighbor as Thyself." As is given in the injunction, "Love the Lord Thy God with all Thine Heart, Thine Soul and Thine Body." In this, as in many, we see upon the physical or earth or material plane the manifestations of that law, without the law itself. With any condition we find as this, which is the manifestation of the opposite from law of love. The gift, the giving, with hope of reward or pay is direct opposition of the law of love. Remember there is no greater than the injunction, "God so loved His Creation, or the World, as to give His Only Begotten Son, for their redemption." Through that love, as man makes it manifest in his own heart and life, does it reach that law, and in compliance of A Law, the law becomes a part of the individual. *That is the law of love.* Giving in action, without the force felt, expressed, manifested, shown, desired or reward for that given. Not that the law of love does away with other laws, but makes *the law of recompense, the law of faith, the law of divine, with the law of earth forces,* if you please, of effect, not defective, but of effect.

So we have *love* is *law, law* is *love. God is love. Love is God.* In that we see the law manifested, not the law itself. Unto the individual, as we have given then, that gets the understanding of self, becomes a part of this. As is found, which come in one, so we have manifestations of the oneness, of the all-ness in love. Now, if we, as individuals, upon the earth

plane, have all of the other elementary forces that make to the bettering
of life, and have not love we are as nothing—nothing. "Though one may
have the gift of prophesy, so as to give great understanding, even of the
graces in Hope, in Charity, in Faith, and has not the law of love in their
heart, soul, mind and though they give their body to give itself for
manifesting even these graces, and has not love they are nothing." In
many, many ways may the manifestations of the law of love be shown,
but without the greater love, even as the Father giveth, even as the soul
giveth, there is no understanding, and no compliance of the forces that
make our later law to this, of effect.

(Q) What is a dream?

(A) There are many various kinds of manifestations that come to an
animate object, or being; that is in the physical plane of man, which the
human family term a *dream*.

Some are produced by suggestions as reach the consciousness of the
physical, through the various forms and manners as these.

When the physical has laid aside the conscious in that region called
sleep, or slumber, when those forces through which the spirit and soul
has manifested itself come, and are reenacted before or through or by
this soul and spirit force, when such an action is of such a nature as to
make or bring back impressions to the conscious mind in the earth or
material plane, it is termed a dream.

This may be enacted by those forces that are taken into the system,
and in the action of digestion that takes place under the guidance of
subconscious forces, become a part of that force through which the
spirit and soul of that entity passed at such time. Such manifestations
are termed or called nightmares, or the abnormal manifestations on the
physical plane of these forces.

In the normal force of dreams are enacted those forces that may be
the fore-shadow of condition, with the comparison by soul and spirit
forces of the condition in *various spheres* through which this soul and
spirit of the given entity has passed in its evolution to the present
sphere. In this age, at present, 1923, [See Background of Reading 3744-2]
there is not sufficient credence given dreams; for the best development
of the human family is to give the greater increase in knowledge of the
subconscious, soul or spirit world. This is a *dream*.

(Q) How should dreams be interpreted?

(A) Depending upon the physical condition of the entity and that which produces or brings the dream to that body's forces.

The better definition of how the interpretation may be best is this: Correlate those Truths that are enacted in each and every dream that becomes a part of this, or the entity of the individual, and use such to the better developing, ever remembering develop means going toward the higher forces, or the Creator.

(Q) Definition of the word evolution with reference to the human family:

(A) Evolution with reference to the human family. Evolution is, as commonly understood by the human family, and upon which there has been much discussion by many peoples, and the question has become one that involves many different phases and meanings to many peoples. Evolution is as reference. In reference to the human family, means rather resuscitation of those forces that have gradually brought man to understand the law of self from within, and by understanding such law has brought the better force in man to bring about the gradual change that has come to man, known through all the ages.

Man was made as man. There was, there is, as we find, only three of the creations as is given, matter force and mind. In each we find that, in the forces as is developed into the conditions, as we find at the present time. All flesh is not of one flesh, but the developing of one has always remained in the same, and has only been to meet the needs of man, for which there was made all that was made, and man's evolving, or evolution, has only been that of the gradual growth upward to the mind of the Maker.

(Q) Is the Darwinian theory of evolution of man right or wrong? Give such an answer as will enlighten the people on this subject of evolution.

(A) Man was made in the beginning, as the ruler over those elements as was prepared in the earth plane for his needs. When the plane became that such as man was capable of being sustained by the forces, and conditions, as were upon the face of the earth plane, man appeared not from that already created, but as the Lord over all that was created, and in man there is found that in the living man, all of that, that may be found without in the whole, whole world or earth plane, and *other* than that, the *soul of man* is that making him above all animal, vegetable, mineral kingdom of the earth plane.

Man *did not* descend from the monkey, but man has evolved, resuscitation, you see, from time to time, time to time, here a little, there a little, line upon line and line and line upon line.

In all ages we find this has been the developing—day by day, day by day, or the evolution as we see from those forces as may be manifested by that, that man has made himself the gradual improvement upon the things made by man, yet made to suffice the needs of certain functioning portions of man's will force, as may be manifested by man, but ever remaining that element to supply that need, whether of sustenance or other functions of man's individual needs, as created by man, this becoming then the exponent of the force as his Creator made him, for the World, and the needs and conditions, man's compliance nearer with those laws brings him gradually to that development necessary to meet the needs of the conditions, place or sphere in which that individual is placed. As in this:

The needs of those in the North Country not the same as those in the Torrid region. Hence development comes to meet the needs in the various conditions under which man is placed. He only using those laws that are ever and ever in existence in the plane, as is given in that of relativity, that being the needs from one relation to another.

The theory is, man evolved, or evolution, from first cause in creation, and brings forth to meet the needs of the man, the preparation for the needs of man has gone down many, many thousands and millions of years, as is known in this plane, for the needs of man in the hundreds and thousands of years to come. Man is man, and God's order of creation, which he represents even as His son, who is the representative of the Father, took on the form of Man, the highest of the creation in the plane, and became to man that element that shows and would show and will show the way, the directing way, the Life, the Water, the Vine, to the everlasting, when guided and kept in that manner and form.

(Q) *Where does the soul come from, and how does it enter the physical body?*

(A) It is already there. "And He breathed into him the breath of life, and he became a living soul", as the breath, the ether from the forces as come into the body of the human when born breathes the breath of life, as it becomes a living soul, provided it has reached that developing in the creation where the soul may enter and find the lodging place.

All souls were created in the beginning, and are finding their way back to whence they came.

(Q) *Where does the soul go when fully developed?*

(A) To its Maker.

2

●

Deeper Views of the Psychic Sense

Text of Reading 900-59 M 30
(Stockbroker, Jewish)

This Psychic Reading given by Edgar Cayce at his office, 322 Grafton Avenue, Dayton, Ohio, this 13th day of April, 1925, in accordance with request made by [900].

PRESENT

Edgar Cayce; Mrs. Cayce, Conductor; Gladys Davis, Steno.

READING

Time of Reading 3:00 P.M. Dayton Time. New York City.

GC: You will have before you the subject matter as was given in psychic state by the body Edgar Cayce, and questions on same as prepared by the enquiring mind of [900]. You will answer these questions as I ask them, in such a manner as to be understood by the mind of [900].

EC: Yes, we have the subject matter here as was given and as transcribed [3744 series]. Ready for questions.

(Q) Explain: "By the suggestion the subconscious may be wavered by the forces

that are brought to bear on the subconscious to reach conscious mind, just as we have in a purely mechanical form." [3744-3]

(A) In the wavering of forces as applied from the subconscious to the conscious mind, first we must take into consideration that conscious mind is of the material world a part. The subconscious mind may only be fully understood when viewed from the spiritual viewpoint or aspect. The conscious mind rarely gains the entrance to truth in the subconscious, save in rest, sleep, or when such consciousnesses are subjugated through the act of the individual, as in the case of Edgar Cayce, through which the subject matter was given. The illustration as given of mechanical way, that is as appearance of stick in water appears bent. When the consciousness views subconscious forces they appear wavered or bended, when viewed from wholly a material viewpoint, whether from the dream in sleep, or viewed by a conscious mind or material mind of truth from trance or from the subconscious condition. Hence in the sleep we may have the superseding appearance of the consciousness and thus waver the appearance of truth obtained, or we may have the suggestion as is given to a mind directing the truth to be obtained from subconscious forces bended in such a manner as to give the wavered aspect to the truth as given. In such a manner, or in one of such manners, then do we see the wavering often (not always) of truths obtained by a consciousness from the subconscious forces. Just as illustrated in the mechanical manner as given in subject matter.

(Q) *It was first given, Soul and Spirit are "forces". Then in illustrating force as given [3744-3]: "That which is the Spirit of any object, animate or inanimate." Explain "Spirit of an object."*

(A) Spirit in an animate object, that giving same life, whether of of that with the attributes of the one, two, three or fourth dimension of same. Spirit in an inanimate object being then that relation as given to same by the mental intelligence of the individual, or person, or thing, giving it a spirit force. As this would be illustrated: To the animal who becomes accustomed to being hitched to a certain post, that post has the spirit for the animal by the mental abilities of the animal's association with same. To man, the stone occupying the place in altar may be of same quarry, of the same strata, of the one occupying the step to the building. The position of one in altar occupying the spirit of reverence.

The one on step occupying the position as of one to reach same. Hence the degrees of the relation as is carried in the inanimate conditions. When this relation then is considered, we see how the evolution, or revelation of same comes to the spirit of the herb, of the fly, of the beast, of the companion. Hence how each occupy their position, or as has been better illustrated in the words as were given, "All flesh is not of one flesh. There are the flesh of animal, of bird, of fishes, of men. There are bodies celestial, bodies terrestrial. The glory of one differs in the glory of another, but because one occupies the exalted position would one do away with that of the uncomely parts? for that which is the uncomely becomes the more comely in its action and self when directed in its proper channel and sphere." Hence we find all occupying then the spirit of that acquired by its position, its relation to other conditions, whether of the animate or inanimate condition and position.

(Q) *What is meant by [3744-3]: "Mental and Physical with relative forces connecting the soul force and unbalancing of the truth may perform on the soul forces that which brings abnormal results to physical and soul matter"?*

(A) Just as has been given in how truth is obtained in the normal or consciousness, may be perverted by the outlook of the individual obtaining same, of as the spirit may view the truth as obtained from a source questionable to the relation of the individual to such conditions. That is, as this: One brought up in the condition of religious liberty does not comprehend a lesson as obtained from one of a faith that would bind the body and the moral and mental forces of an individual, the same as one would understand such lesson brought up in that faith, or as would be seen in this: All religious faiths have their element of truth. Would be hard for the Christian faith to understand the lesson of the Mohammedan faith, and each may gain the lesson to its own destruction, for the relation of each truth bears its relativity of force to the developing of the entity. Then we return to the same premise. What may be viewed by the entity in that plane of the two square, or two fold, or two quantity life, cannot understand the vision of one having reached the threefold or three quantity life.

(Q) *Explain the different environments which the individual enters before reaching the earth plane, while in earth plane and after.*

(A) The individual entity before coming in earth's plane bears only the spirit relation to the Universal Forces, with a soul to be made, through the environments of Creation, equal to the Created, given the free will as to how same shall be developed. Before entering the earth's plane of its own choice, or free will, developing through those spheres it chooses for its developing. In the earth's plane and spheres then becoming subject to the laws of that sphere to which it chooses its sojourn, passing through same with its urge of development taken on in the beginning, subject to the environment though which it passes for its development, and as has been given, all soul and spirit force is of the Creator, and given to the individual, which brings or makes it an individual to use as it sees fit. As illustrated in that given by Him that shows the Way, the talents given to every entity those of its making, by its use, all being the same in the beginning. As the developing passes, the entity, the nearer the whole becomes one with the Creator, the nearer comes the perfect developing, for the whole law is to be one with the Creator. Yet never losing its identity, for that given in the beginning, but becoming one with the Creator as each unit of the blood itself the portion of the earthly being in its sojourn through the earth. We find in the Man the every elements and representation of how the entity one with the Creator, and with the Will to make same one with the Creator, with all the attributes of a creator, and with the will to make same one with Him, or rebel against that element.

We are through for the present.

Text of Reading 900-19 M 29

This Psychic Reading given by Edgar Cayce at the Cambridge Hotel, Apt. 106, 60 West 68th Street, New York City, New York, this 15th day of January, 1925, in accordance with request made by [900].

P R E S E N T

Edgar Cayce; [900], Conductor; Gladys Davis, Steno. Mrs. Edgar Cayce & Mrs. Freda Blumenthal.

R E A D I N G

Time of Reading . . . Street, 6:10 P.M. New York Time. New York City, N.Y.

[900]: You will have before you the subject matter in book as given in readings, particularly subject matter on Psychic Phenomena and on Mind, [3744]. [See 900-19] You will also have before you the analysis of this subject matter as written by the body [900] in a book which he now holds in his hand, present in this room. You will tell us if this analysis is correct, and give that additional subject matter which will make the chapter on Psychic Phenomena and Mind better understood by the body and mind of [900], present in this room. You will answer questions regarding this.

EC: Yes, we have the data here, as has been transcribed and written, and that also as has been written by [900], present in this room. This data, as we find, and the explanation of same, are very good, and only need specific questions and answers in given places, that same may be complete, readable and acceptable to those who are students of phenomena of like character.

(Q) Explain the following [See 3744-2]: "Psychic, in the broader sense, meaning spirit, soul, or imagination of the mind when attuned to the various phases of either of these two portions of the entity of an individual, or from the entity of others who are passed into other planes than the physical or material."

(A) As we have in this: We reason with the material mind. We have those accepted facts and conditions, for the material mind must have a premise, or basis, in which all agree. When we find the action of any given premise, performing same is phenomena. When such action relates to the mind of a body (human we are speaking of), such is then a form of psychic, or mental, or mind force, or phenomena. Same as we have when there is that projection from the spirit forces, as is manifest, and as is an accepted fact or premise. This action upon the material world (see, just opposite from that given) is the psychic phenomena, and is given from this condition as asked. There is both the mental phenomena, the soul phenomena, the spiritual phenomena. All psychic phenomena, for psychic means of the mind, in the accepted term. Then, as we see manifestations of any of the conditions that relate to the physical mind the portion of soul entity belonging to physical, the portion of the spiritual belonging to physical, we see the phenomena, or the psychic phenomena, manifested in a material world, whether projected from the world into mental space, or from spirit world into the mental or material world. Keep each separate. Correlate each in its form of projection, that applicable to the needs of the human family, to bring those conditions, whether of the physical, mental or spiritual, that gives the better understanding of man's relation to man, and man's relation to Maker. Give those conditions that others may understand and benefit thereby. There is no condition existing in a world as the earth plane but what there is the phenomena in every action of psychic forces manifesting. As we find, the projection then of such conditions should be correlated under their various heads, and each carried to their bounds, that there may be the more perfect understanding, and not confuse the mental projection with spirit projection, or injection, into the material world. Spirit is the life–giving force in every condition, whether of mental or material action. Whatever force is acted upon has its attributes, the same as we find in all life–producing element. Whenever the element reaches that stage where it, the element, is able to give or reproduce self, we see the manifestation of the spirit force, modified by that element's own attributes, even from the lowest form of life to the highest. When we have the physical body of the lord of creation, man, we find all such conditions manifest through that body; the mind being that element that directs and makes man the master of the condition, situation, or creation. The soul [is] the element, that given to man that man may be one with the Creator. Hence the developing of that portion that becomes the spiritual element, that it may be made one with the Creator. Hence we see from the lowest to the highest the manifestations of psychic phenomena in the material world. Hence we have the psychic phenomena of the lower animal kingdom, of the mineral kingdom, of the plant kingdom, of the animal kingdom as advanced, and as then becomes the man's condition, position. Hence we find the evolution of the soul, as has been given, and as is manifest in the material world, took place before man's appearance, the evolution of the soul in the mind of the Creator, not in the material world.

(Q) *What form, or how can the conscious mind conceive of this soul in a human entity, and then in the spirit plane, after the physical has returned to earth?*

(A) We have the soul as the body of the spiritual force manifested in the individual, as we find in every body animated with the ability to reproduce in self a thing separate from the rest of the world, yet depending upon the material world for sustenance, the same as we have in the soul, as given, and separate entity, the dwelling or indwelling in man, is that dependence upon the attributes of the body that it possesses for that necessary for its development. Hence the conditions as regard its developing, depending both upon the environment and upon the hereditary conditions, considered from the physical only. Hence the relative attraction for conditions of the soul for that necessary development of that soul from entity to entity, whether material or spiritual.

(Q) *How are projections received from spiritual entities in the next plane?*

(A) As each entity in the earth plane, or material plane, or flesh plane manifestation, such entity (material now we are speaking of) leaves with that relative conditions about the environment that spiritual force as manifest in that entity; when such an entity has left the material plane, or laid aside the carnal conditions, the body then, we have that spiritual entity in the spiritual plane. The spiritual entity possesses that element as is known, or called, in the earth plane, or material plane, the subconsciousness. The subconsciousness is awakened in material plane through an attunement, through such attunement there may be projections from one to the other.

(Q) *What form does the spirit entity take, or explain -*

(A) Taking that form that the entity creates for itself in the plane in which the existence is passed. As we have in the earth's plane the imagination, the mind of the individual pictures to itself, through its carnal relations, that condition to which its individual relation of entity assumes to itself, and the entity possessing that same ability to assume that position in which it may manifest itself according to its relative position to that merited condition in its existence.

(Q) *Explain the plane of spirit and soul forces, and what relation this plane has to earth. You will start with death, as we know it.*

(A) In that moment—as in birth we have the beginning of an earthly sojourn, little or long, as time may be—as the birth into the spiritual plane begins with the death in earth plane; merely the separation of the spiritual and soul forces from the earthly connections.

We are through for the present.

Text of Reading 900-21 M 29

This Psychic Reading given by Edgar Cayce at the Cambridge Hotel, Apt. 103, 60 West 68th Street, New York City, New York, on this 16th day of January, 1925, in accordance with request made by [900].

PRESENT

Edgar Cayce; [900], Conductor; Gladys Davis, Steno. Mrs. Edgar Cayce, Mrs. Freda Blumenthal, Mr. & Mrs. Edwin Blumenthal, Dr. Berger, Mr. Biddlecome.

READING

Time of Reading 10:00 P.M. New York Time. New York City, New York.

[900]: Now you have before you the book on subject matter, written by the body, Edgar Cayce, in the subconscious condition, in the hand of [900], present in this room. You will also have before you the outline of this book, written by the body, [900], also in the body, [900]'s hand, present in this room. You will answer questions, so as to clarify the book on subject matter [3744] to the mind of [900].

EC: Yes, we have the subject matter here, as transcribed and written. Also the explanation on subject matter as written by the body, [900]. We have in this subject matter many conditions that may be clarified by questions. Ready for questions.

(Q) Explain "Mind is the factor that is in direct opposition to will."

(A) We have many phases of mind. We have the mind of the spirit consciousness, of the physical sub–conscious, or soul. We have the mind of the physical body, through which any or all of these may manifest. The will [is] that active principle against which such manifestations re-spond. Hence [it is in] direct opposition to mind action. This, we find then, refers to the condition in the material world, will, see? The will in the spiritual plane, or spirit consciousness (not spirit entity) being the creation of that manifested in the earth plane. Hence the different con-ditions in will's manifesting and in how will [is in] opposition to the mind forces.

(Q) Explain "Mind is a factor as senses are of the mind, and as the soul and spirit *are factors of the entity, one in all, all in one."*

(A) As has been given. These conditions, mind of the soul, mind of the physical body, mind of the spiritual entity, are separated, that one may gain the knowledge of its action. As we have then the mind of the spiritual entity, that mind wherein the entity (spiritual entity [we are] speaking of) manifests in the spiritual plane, the mind in the physical body the subconscious, the conscious, through which the entity manifests in the physical world, one in all, all in one. In one in the spiritual mind, acted upon by their attributes, principally will, for it is the factor in the physical world, in the spiritual world, for the action being that through which the manifestations of any factor known. As we would have in this: Knowledge comes through the senses in the physical body to the conscious mind. The subconscious has the storing of the knowledge of given conditions; when the consciousness receives through the sense that knowledge, the will [is] the action against the incentives set forth.

(Q) *Explain how the mind serrogates [segregates?], correlates, or divides the impressions to the portion needed to develop the entity, or physical force, toward the spark or infinite force, giving the life force to the body.*

(A) In this, again we have the manifestations of physical conditions that may be manifest in a physical body, and conditions that may be manifest in the spiritual body. As we have in correlation of conditions that assist in the building, the developing, in the physical body, the entity, the inmost being, the expectancy of the physical body must be awakened before the body, through its tissue, its vital forces, can emanate the necessary building, or eliminating forces, of the physical body, to rebuild or develop properly. Hence the cause of death in physical world. The lack of the consciousness of the indwelling spiritual force in the spiritual entity in physical body. The breaking, the division, in the portions. Hence the disintegration of physical to the birth in the spiritual. As we have again in the physical the correlation of those elements necessary for the setting in motion of those vibrations to create the offspring, the developing begins with the separation of those elements in the physical body to create physical body, born into physical world. The knowledge of the spiritual forces begins the development through the awakening of the spiritual forces in the entity. Hence the birth into the spiritual world. Hence the necessity of the rebirth in and through such conditions, until the whole [is] made in the will of the Creator.

(Q) *Explain what the divide between the soul and spiritual forces is? How manifest, and how we may study self to gain the approach to that divide.*

(A) This [is] of the spiritual entity in its entirety. The super-conscious [is] the divide, that one-ness lying between the soul and the spirit force, within the spiritual entity. Not of earth forces at all, only awakened with the spiritual indwelling and acquired individually.

(Q) *How may the individual think, study, and act to acquire this awakening?*

(A) Study to show thyself approved unto Him, rightly dividing the words of truth, keeping self unspotted from the world, avoiding the appearance of evil, for as is given, those who would seek God must believe that He *is*, and a rewarder of those who would seek Him. That is, that the Creator has that One-ness with the individual to make that One-ness with Him. As is given in the conditions as is manifest through those who would seek the One-ness with God, for only those who have approached sufficient to make the mind of the physical, the mind of the soul, the mind of the spiritual, One with Him, may understand or gather that necessary to approach that understanding.

(Q) *Explain, "the only real life being that which in the material or physical plane is called psychic."*

(A) This we find has been given in explanation of psychic.

We are through for the present.

Text of Reading 900-22 M 29

This Psychic Reading given by Edgar Cayce at the Cambridge Hotel, Apt. 103, 60 West 68th Street, New York City, New York, this 17th day of January, 1925, in accordance with request made by [900].

PRESENT

Edgar Cayce; [900], Conductor; Gladys Davis, Steno. Mr. & Mrs. Edwin Blumenthal.

READING

Time of Reading 2:10 P.M. New York Time. New York City, N.Y.

[900]: Now you will have before you the reading given on the 16th day of January, 1925, [900–21] on the subject matter of the book [3744], written by Edgar Cayce in the psychic condition, and the analysis made by the body, [900], on this book. You will continue to answer questions on this matter.

EC: Yes, we have the subject matter as transcribed here, and the enquiring mind of [900], relative to such subject matter. These subject matters, we find, are the explanation as of subject matter given in book, and are in keeping with that intent and purpose that the enquiring mind of each entity may gain the better knowledge of self, or in other words, what it's all about anyway. Ready for questions.

(Q) *What is meant by souls within this sphere may be communicated with by the body, Edgar Cayce, in the psychic state?*

(A) Each and every soul entity, or earthly entity, passing through the earth's plane, radiates in that plane those conditions that are radiated from the soul or spiritual entity in the individual. This, then, becomes the fact, the real fact, in the material world. When the body, Edgar Cayce, in the psychic or subconscious condition, is able then to reach all the subconscious minds, when directed to such subconscious minds by suggestion, whether in the material world or in the spiritual world, provided the spiritual entity has not passed entirely into that condition where the radiation, or the relative forces, are superseded by other radiations. Then we only reach those radiations left in earth's plane that are taken again when entering in earth's plane, whether entity [is] conscious of same or not. The consciousness of reaching that condition wherein the physical body may take up that truth known, must be reached by all. Hence the given expression, the body, Edgar Cayce, in the subconscious condition, may communicate with those passed into the spiritual plane.

(Q) *In reality, then, the body, Edgar Cayce, in the psychic state, communicates with thoughts, and not with the spiritual entities themselves.*

(A) With the thoughts, and with the radiation as is given. Then we have as the illustration of this condition in the body, [900]. We have, when this entity enters the subconscious, through the medium of laying aside the conscious mind, and the projection of the spiritual guide, the father, the thoughts, the impressions, as would be given by that entity, entering the subconsciousness of [900]. Not the spiritual entity's taking form, save in the subconsciousness of [900].

(Q) Then, may the body, [900], his spiritual guide recede to that point, or position, where the body, [900], may no longer receive those radiations?

(A) Not until [900] supersedes those radiations by creations in radiations of his own, for thoughts are deeds, and all conditions remain, as given.

(Q) Are those radiations like a vibratory force on our earth's plane, such as light wave?

(A) May be compared to same, but of the spiritual radiation, and not material radiation; that is, those radiations as come from spirit form may take form in vibratory radiation of color, or light, through the individual's attunement.

(Q) Is the spiritual guide conscious of the communication with the earthly body?

(A) When the spiritual entity so desires, it may. That entity has its own condition to receive.

(Q) Explain persona, its form, character and evolution.

(A) Persona, that radiation through the individual in the earth plane as received by its development through the spiritual planes, as we would have in this: We find two entities in an earth plane, of same environment, of same hereditary conditions. One with a personality, or persona, radiating from every thought or action. The other submerging every other persona it may contact. Different degree of development. Persona comes from development, then, either in earth plane or spiritual plane. The persona [is] acquired physically, the persona [is a] natural development. This condition we find comes nearer to the radiation in astrological condition, for partakes of the environment of spheres or universal action in the developing entity. Hence we find persons born under certain solar conditions have that condition of persona that radiates in the same direction, while the individual conditions as brought to, or given off from such persona, may be of entirely a different nature, for these are of the different developments. As we find, that would be illustrated in conditions of individuals born in the material world, on the same moment. One in East, one in West. The different environment under which the persona would manifest would partake of that environment, yet there would be similar conditions in the earth plane to each entity.

(Q) What is meant by mental and physical, with relative forces connecting the soul force, and unbalancing of the truth may perform on the soul forces that which brings abnormal results to physical and soul matter?

(A) An entity, knowing in self the results of certain psychological, physiological, or mental conditions, yet with material will vibrating or giving that directly opposed to the condition. These bring the conditions to the mental, the soul forces, of the body at an advarience [which are at variance] to the truth. This we find is manifest in many an individual in the earth plane, or as would be termed, [they] see the truth, but [are] too hardheaded to accept it.

We are through for the present.

Text of Reading 900-23 M 29

This psychic reading given by Edgar Cayce at the Cambridge Hotel, Apt. 106, 60 West 68th Street, New York City, New York, on this 18th day of January, 1925, in accordance with request made by [900].

PRESENT

Edgar Cayce; [900], Conductor; Gladys Davis, Steno. Mrs. Edgar Cayce, Mrs. Freda Blumenthal.

READING

Time of Reading 1:30 P.M. New York Time. New York City, N.Y.

[900]: Now you will have before you the Book on Subject Matter, [3744] written by the body, Edgar Cayce, in the psychic state, and the analysis of this book, written by the body, [900] present in this room. You will also have the enquiring mind of this body. You will continue with questions on this subject matter.

EC: The subject matter, we have the condition here, as transcribed and given by Edgar Cayce, analysis of same as written by [900], and the enquiring mind. This subject matter as written, and the analysis of same very good, giving the better understanding in the physical or material plane of conditions relating to those pertaining to the spiritual forces.

Ready for questions.

(Q) What is meant by environments carried on to the reentering of the entity?

(A) In this specific place, meant that relating to the body, Edgar Cayce, in the psychic state, and the environment of the mind questioning and following the questions and answers given. In the broader sense, this means the environment creating in the mind the mentality of the physical body in earth's plane, and furnishing that upon which the soul, so to speak, feeds upon, and being the environment as would be the companion of the soul in the spiritual sphere. For, as we find in the spiritual entity the subconscious, the physical world becomes the conscious, in the spiritual, and that known in the physical as the super–conscious, as the subconscious in the spiritual sphere. Hence that entity in the spiritual sphere reaches the developments as attained through the environments, reaching from one sphere to another, as would be given in this: Not who would ascend into heaven to bring God to earth, or who would descend into the depths to bring him up, for He is ever near, within each own heart.

Then, as we see, environment brings this condition in the development of an entity, through the physical or material sphere. We find and entity in the spiritual sphere entering in the material sphere, in that condition necessary for the entity's development in the material sphere. The environments about that entity becoming the portions in the subconscious that the soul and spirit feeds upon, or develops through, by the action upon in the spiritual sphere of the spiritual understanding of conditions. Hence an entity in the physical that lives more in the subconscious is spoken of as a spiritual minded individual.

(Q) *Make clear what is meant by "in that of the spirit and soul forces thought and memory are as the entity."*

(A) This, as we find, comes in that condition wherein a material entity may wonder whether thought in memory, or memory thought, for we find that the indwelling of the subconscious forces, in the spiritual entity, entering the material planes, bring gradually the thought of the development necessary for the entity's development towards the higher realm. Hence where will again enters into the condition of being the opposition of soul and spirit forces. For we find, when thought would take the possession if the inmost soul or being of an entity, that this is as of memory necessary for development of entity; when such conditions are willfully banished for the lighter conditions, that would remove the necessary environment, for development, the body is exercising thought and memory by will's forces. Not that any entity should enter into any condition that would so unbalance the mind (conscious we are speaking of), as to bring upon itself condemnation but rather that, that will make the balanced mind. For the bringing of condemnation from other minds becomes environment in the mind itself. Separate these. Correlate these as truths given here, for this is the basis of heredity and environment. Break not the will of an entity, rather guide, guard and direct same in those channels through the development, for we all must pay the price necessary for development of self. Hence, never give to an entity a dictum, for that entity. Rather outline that as found in self, and let others apply same to self. For the mind partakes of memory and thought of its own, and takes that necessary for its own development. For, as has been given, think not to stand alone. Immediately given, think not to induce others to think as self.

(Q) *Correlate that just given directly to the body, [900], to recent events.*

(A) That in the memory of the body [900], correlated with self's development and thoughts on same, relate in this manner: Give thought in self as to conditions that have arisen, for they relate to the thoughts of the individual, [900], and when reached in the subconscious again, which will occur on the 21st, the mind will attain that understanding; yet do not give those thoughts to others, or attempt to force others to think as self, for they do not. We are relating all known development, for we have passed into the subconscious action in a material world. [See 900-26]

(Q) *Give us the relation of evolution and thought transferences. How may thought transference be developed?*

(A) Just as has been described, when related to many individuals, we find that when thought of many individuals are directed to one focusing point, the condition becomes accentuated by force—see?—of thought manifested. In evolution, we find the development as has been just given, in the correlation of the human mind and soul, toward perfection. Just so the evolution of the soul came in the attributes of God Mind, and given in Man. As thoughts are directed, the transmission of thought waves gradually becomes the reality, just as light and heat waves in material world are now used by man. Just to in the spiritual planes, the elements of thought transmission, or transference, may become real. Be sure of this fact, and assured of same. Thought transference occurs when both bodies, or entities, are in the subconscious condition, whether for a moment, or whether for ages, for time in spiritual forces is not as in material forces.

We are through for the present.

Text of Reading 900-24 M 29

This Psychic Reading given by Edgar Cayce at the Cambridge Hotel, Apt. 103, 60 West 68th Street, New York City, New York, this 18th day of January, 1925, in accordance with request made by [900].

P R E S E N T

Edgar Cayce; [900], Conductor; Gladys Davis, Steno. Mrs. Freda Blumenthal, Mr. & Mrs. Edwin Blumenthal, Dr. Kraus, and Hugh Lynn Cayce.

R E A D I N G

Time of Reading 7:00 P.M. New York Time. New York City, New York.

[900]: You will have before you the two books, one written by the body, Edgar Cayce, in a psychic state [3744], the other an analysis of that book by the body, [900], present in this room. You will have before you the enquiring mind of the body, [900], and will answer questions as relating to this subject matter, so as to be understandable by the mind of this body.

EC: Yes, we have the data here, and the analysis of same, with the enquiring mind of [900]. The analysis as written, as has been given, is such as to make the subject matter more understandable to those seeking the information upon such subject matter, for we find the mind as gives that interpretation in the analysis correlates with the data as given, for as has been given, the body, the mind of [900], has that ability to give that explanation in the physical forces, as such may be understood to other minds. Ready for questions.

(Q) *Explain in detail the law of relativity.*

(A) This law of relativity we find, as has been given, relates to the law as was set in motion in the beginning, when the Universe as a whole came into existence.

As related to the mind, and to the earth conditions, we find first beginning with that of the earth in its position, with the other elements about same. These became the law of the relative position regarding the spheres, and as there begun the lowest form of the animal and mineral, and vegetable, forces in the earth, we begun with all relative condition regarding those conditions from other spheres, and their relations to same.

In the mind, then, and the soul forces as was given in man, in his creation, bears its relation then to all other forces in the Universe, and as man's mind developed in the earth's forces, the seeking to find those relations still remaining that relative force as exercised in an earth plane; each bearing its relation to the other, just as the planetary system is to earth and its relation to each and every kingdom as presented itself in its relation to the earth condition, and to those of the Creator and the Created, and as we find, then, in the soul's development to reach that plane wherein the whole entity may become one with that creative forces, that creative energy, that Oneness with the God, this we find needs then that development through all the planes in the Universal Forces, or throughout the Universe. Hence the necessity of developing in that plane. All bearing, then, the relative condition, position, action, state of being, to that creative force, and that created.

As we would have, as is shown in the earth's plane from the elements about the earth, all combination in chemical form begins a form of condition with force, less the creative plasm of the entity, the being, to give reproduction in itself, that energy, that first force, that spirit agent; in such being the relative force to all life giving forces. Hence, in its development, each bearing its relation, and its relative relation, to those conditions upon which the existence of such force depends.

(Q) *Have the lower forms of creation, such as animals, should, or [do they have] any life in the spirit plane?*

(A) All have the spirit force. The man, as made, carrying the soul force, that made equal with the Creator in the beginning, in that of relative production in its (man's) plane of existence. Hence the necessity of development of that soul energy. Only when reached in that of the man, do we find the soul complete in the earth's entities, for in man we find both the spirit entity and the physical entity, as we see exemplified in this body, mind, here of [900].

(Q) *What is meant by position as an attribute to the soul?*

(A) That meaning, in this instance as given, as of the relative position of the development of the soul through the earth's plane, in which it manifests the development attained in relative positions in the spheres through which the soul passes.

(Q) *Explain, "So those things that do appear to have reality, and their reality to the human mind, have in reality passed into past conditions before they have reached the mind, for with the earth's laws and its relation to other spheres has man become a past condition."*

(A) This relates to that of the spiritual law in its relative forces in the earth planes, or that of a finite mind attempting to comprehend the laws of the infinite mind, for before *any* condition exists in the finite mind, it has become a past condition, relatively spoken, from the infinite mind. As we have in the earth's sphere, when the light from the planets, or any of the elements in solar system, cast their shadow, or light, upon the earth's element, for such conditions have passed into space before it can be a conscious condition to the human consciousness. Again the relative conditions in the earth's plane, or sphere, as related to the spiritual conditions, or laws, for as would again be sought, one who would understand the infinite mind must approach that with the finite in such condition as to receive that spiritual insight into such relations, must less conditions.

(Q) *How may the conscious mind be brought to this condition?*

(A) The conscious mind *cannot* be brought to this condition.

(Q) *Explain "The destiny of man lies within the sphere or scope of the planets."*

(A) That each and every entity passes through the sphere or scope, or plane, of each planet, and each existence must have its relation to such an entity.

(Q) *Explain how, why, and in what manner, planets influence an individual at birth?*

(A) As the entity is born into the earth's plane, the relation to that planet, or that sphere, from which the spirit entity took its flight, or its position, to enter the earth plane, has the greater influence in the earth's plane. Just as the life lived in the earth's plane directs to what position the spirit entity takes in the sphere.

(Q) *What is meant by "influence of the planets in and about earth's plane is deficient?"*

(A) In this relation, as given, that as has been generally taught in times past, not the existent conditions from the spirit plane.

We are through.

Text of Reading 900-25 M 29

This Psychic Reading given by Edgar Cayce at his office, 322 Grafton Avenue, Dayton, Ohio, this 21st day of January, 1925, in accordance with request made by [900].

PRESENT

Edgar Cayce; Gertrude Cayce, Conductor; Gladys Davis, Steno.

READING

Time of Reading 322 Grafton Ave., 12:00 Noon Dayton Time. Dayton, Ohio.

GC: You will have before you the subject matter [3744] as was given in psychic state by the body, Edgar Cayce, and questions on same as prepared by the enquiring mind of [900]. You will answer these questions as I ask them, in such a manner as to be understood by this mind of [900].

EC: Yes, we have that subject matter as transcribed and given by Edgar Cayce while in the subconscious state, and the enquiring mind of [900] regarding such information in subject matter. Ready for questions, regarding same.

(Q) *Explain and illustrate, "In the spheres of many of the planets, within the same solar system, we find they are banished to certain conditions in the developing about the sphere from which they pass, and again, and again, and again return from one to another, until they are prepared to meet the everlasting Creator of our entire Universe, of which our system is only a small part."*

(A) In this condition, we find much as is given in Relativity of Force.

In this, again we find in this: The entity entering the earth's plane, and manifesting in the flesh, when such conditions are shown in the body that the spiritual entity is banished unto Saturn, that condition in the earth's solar system to which all insufficient matter is cast for the remoulding, as it were, for its passage through the development in earth's plane, or in the spheres to which the earth's relations adhere in the development of a spiritual or physical body. In this we find the relations as given from those spheres in the earth's sphere; that is, as in Mercury, as in Venus, as in Mars, as in Jupiter, as in Earth, as in Uranus, as in Neptune, and the chancing, or changing, as it were, from one development to another, until the entity passes from that solar system, or sphere, through Arcturus or Septimus, as we see. As would be illustrated in this: We find in the earth's plane that entity that manifests such hate, such aggrandizement of the laws of the flesh, in any desire made unnatural. These find their reclamation, their remoulding, their beginning again, in the spheres of Saturn's relative forces. Hence again pass through those spheres in which the entity (spiritual) must manifest, that it (the entity) may manifest the gained development through the earth's plane. For in flesh must the entity manifest, and make the will One with the God, or Creative Force, in the Universe, and as such development reaches that plane, wherein the development may pass into other spheres and systems, of which our (the earth's) solar system is only a small part; in this, then, is meant the entity must develop in that sphere until it (the entity) has reached that stage wherein it may manifest through the spiritual planes, as would be called from the relation to physical or fleshly plane.

(Q) *Explain that barrier between conscious and subconscious mind. How may we eliminate it to allow the subconscious to direct?*

(A) As would best be illustrated in this: We (individuals) find in the earth's plane those mental conditions wherein the conscious and subconscious would manifest by some given suggestion. The entity, through will, reasons with the condition. Hence the barrier as created. Again, we have as exemplified, or shown, in this: Any indiscreet condition, as regarding the mental development, that would be made as to submerge the subconscious forces, then the barrier that would bring the direct condition in the given condition. As we find when the mental forces are in that condition of submerging the conscious forces, the entity attempting to create the consciousness of the transition, creates barrier. As we would find illustrated in these conditions: As the physical body sinks into that state wherein slumber of the physical body takes hold of physical conditions, and the body becomes submerged into the earthly subconscious, the continual thought as is carried, to see physical reaction, creates barrier.

Now, to overcome such conditions, bring about the consciousness, the One-ness of Mind, Soul and Body, that when such submerged conditions are enacted, we find the subconscious takes the direction in the physical plane. Then such an entity is given, as spiritual minded, subconscious minded, subconscious directed, spiritual directed individuals. The more this becomes manifested, the more the entity may gain the impressions, the actual conditions of the subconscious forces, those ever directing, that gives the light and development to the soul's forces from the physical plane.

(Q) Explain, *"All the elements that go to make up the expressions reached to the mental forces of an individual, are actions of the psychic forces from another individual, and is [are] the collaboration of truth as found in the individual, or entity, expressing or manifesting itself, one with the other."*

(A) In this, we find that as giving how that each entity gains the impressions through the transmission of impressions, one toward another, and when the elements in the entity are such as the mental forces (speaking of see?) allow the suggestions from such entity, the collaboration, the mental impressions, depressions, the mental forces, give then that expression to the individual and find the lodgement in which the mental will build, as we would find illustrated in this: Though an entity in the earth plane may be adverse [averse?] to conditions, a mental mind of another individual may so picture conditions of that directly opposed to the mental development of the other individual [that] those collaborations may become such as to be wavered, as to be given the truth, or be given the untruth, for we are giving then of physical conditions alone, and not seeking the collaboration through the spiritual or the subconscious forces, and we find through such chasms, through such elements, comes the mental development, the soul development, the ability of each entity to take that necessary for that soul's development, and in this manner do we find collaboration of truths, collaboration of every thought coming to each and every entity, for "Thoughts are Deeds," and carry that impression that acts through the individual entity.

(Q) *Explain in detail further soul and spirit forces becoming as one force, and manifesting their force and workings to the physical plane, by securing information from subconscious minds presented, or reflections of impressions left by those who have gone to next plane.*

(A) With the perfect understanding of any law, the law may be made a part of the entity, and as the development through the physical plane is to gain the understanding of all Universal Laws, the knowledge thus attained and made a part of the entity, brings the development, whether from those still in earth plane, whether from subconscious conditions, or from those who have left their impressions in the earth plane, and have passed to other planes. Hence the necessity of the given force as was said, "My Son, in all Thy getting, get understanding", and the ability to apply same.

We are through for the present.

Text of Reading 900-31 M 29

This Psychic Reading given by Edgar Cayce at his office, 322 Grafton Avenue, Dayton, Ohio, this 4th day of February, 1925, in accordance with request made by [900].

PRESENT

Edgar Cayce; Gertrude Cayce, Conductor; Gladys Davis, Steno.

READING

Time of Reading 3:45 P.M. Dayton Time. New York City, N.Y.

GC: You will give two readings at this time. After you have finished with the first, you will say, "We have finished with this reading," at which time I will give you the suggestions necessary for the second. You will have before you the book [3744 series] written by Edgar Cayce in the psychic state, and the transcribed edition the body, [900], . . . Street, is now writing. You will have before you his mind and the intense study he is making to re-write this book, and as he is now working on the chapter of Mind, you will clarify his understanding on this subject, so that he may write clearly and in a manner comprehensible for others who read his work. You will answer questions.

EC: Yes, we have the data as transcribed, and the mind, [900], pertaining to the writing attempted to be done. Ready for questions.

(Q) *Explain and illustrate the difference in the faculties of Mind, Subconscious and Superconscious.*

(A) The superconscious mind being that of the spiritual entity, and in action only when the subconscious is become the conscious mind. The subconscious being the superconscious of the *physical* entity, partaking then of the soul forces, and of the material plane, as acted upon through and by mental mind. Hence the developing in the physical plane through environment being that as is given to the soul forces in subconscious mind to live upon. Illustrated, as has been given, in the light as came to Saul on way to Damascus. The superconsciousness of Jesus came to the subconscious of Saul, yet he could not retain in conscious that necessary for him to do. The superconscious came to that of him directed to act in the conscious manner, or Saul, as he continued in the subconscious, seeking for the light of that he could not make clear to his consciousness.

(Q) *Is it correct for [900] to say in his book that the superconsciousness is the mind or supreme controlling force of the Universal Forces?*

(A) As pertaining to an individual, yes. As pertaining to Universal Forces, in the larger sense, no, but through the superconscious the Universal Forces are made active in subconsciousness. As is illustrated in the work as done through body, Edgar Cayce: Through consciousness the suggestion to the subconscious forces appertain to those conditions of the superconscious of the individual, coming then in touch with the Universal Forces in that manner and channel, for as the spiritual entity in its development has been in and partaken of the Universal Forces, in its development, the entity, when submerged from physical to that of superconscious and subconscious, appertain to those elements, and of that element the superconsciousness a portion of the great Universal Forces.

(Q) *Do animals have the faculty of mind known as subconscious?*

(A) No. The mind of the animal is as pertaining to the conditions that would bring the continuation of species and of foods, and in that manner all in the animal kingdom; pertaining then, Mind and Spirit; man reaching that development wherein the soul becomes the individual that may become the companion, and One with the Creator.

(Q) An animal has sense, remembrance, and the higher animals obey orders. How?

(A) Just as has been given, or as has been seen. In the first was given man and mind [to] subdue the earth in every element. As given, again all manner of animal in the earth, in the air, under the sea, has been tamed of man, yet the man himself has not reached that wherein he may perfectly control himself, save making the will One with the Creator, as man makes the will of the animal one with his. The control then in trained animals being the projection in man. The trained mind of those in natural state, the element as given, Spirit and Mind, the specie keep life.

(Q) Explain the difference between experience as in an animal and experience as in man, as related to Mind.

(A) In animal is that as appertains to the consciousness of the animal mind, with spirit. As in man, that is of consciousness co-related with man's development, or the higher elements of mind and of matter. Hence man developed, becomes lord and master over animal kingdom. Man degraded becomes the companion, the equal with the beast, or the beastly man. Then we would find this illustrated as in this: Experience to man gives the understanding through the subconscious obtaining the remembrance. The animal only the animal forces, as would be found in this: Fire to man is ever dread, to an animal only by sense of smell does it know the difference. The experience does not lead it away.

We are through with this reading.

Text of Reading 900-56 M 30
(Stockbroker, Jewish)

This Psychic Reading given by Edgar Cayce at his office, 322 Grafton Avenue, Dayton, Ohio, this 7th day of April, 1925, in accordance with request made by [900].

P R E S E N T

Edgar Cayce; Mrs. Cayce, Conductor; Gladys Davis, Steno.

R E A D I N G

Time of Reading 11:40 A.M. Dayton Time. New York City.

GC: You will have before you, as I read same, the manuscript as prepared by [900], on Psychic Phenomena [based on the 3744 series]. You will make such corrections in same as will be in keeping with the truth of such phenomena as viewed by the Forces of Edgar Cayce while in the Psychic State. I will read a whole page of this, and when I stop you will make the corrections as outlined, and when you have finished with that page you will so state.

EC: No corrections to be made as here.

(A) Instead of "gain that power" acquired that power. The difference in these being, one is as of meted out, the other is as of merited.

(A) No corrections, save this might be added, or may not be added. The gift or the gained psychic force may be abused, the same as any of the senses of the physical body, and through abuse of same may bring destructive forces to the individual in the physical and in the spiritual life.

(A) We have no corrections to make with this portion.

(A) (Interruption). We are conscious of the action of psychic and spiritual forces in the same manner we are conscious of the action of electrical forces in any manner in the physical world, or as we see, "The wind bloweth where it listeth. Thou heareth the sound thereof though know of from whence it cometh nor whence it goeth." The electrical vibration of man's direction we may reach the action, yet no one fathoms the force, the direction of the applied force. All becoming under one law, and are of the law pertaining to psychic force and psychic vibration as are manifested in the material world. We recognize the vibratory forces in electrical forces, and such are weighed, measured, and in those of radio forces we have electrical vibration magnifying the vibrations as are set forth in same. The same we have in spirit or psychic or mind vibration. These are magnified by the action on those in attune with that vibration. (Reading)

Correct. No corrections other than given.

(A) No corrections. May be some expanding as regards the conditions of the birth into the spirit plane and to gain the spiritual consciousness as is reached in that plane and the bringing of the spiritual consciousness, as reaching that dimension as is set forth in the first chapters, first portion in this.

(A) No corrections.

We are through for the present.

Text of Reading 900-66 M 30
(Stockbroker, Jewish)

This psychic reading given by Edgar Cayce at his office, 322 Grafton Avenue, Dayton, Ohio, this 6th day of May, 1925, in accordance with request made by self—[900].

PRESENT

Edgar Cayce; Mrs. Cayce, Conductor; Gladys Davis, Steno.

READING

Time of Reading 3:20 P.M. Dayton Savings Time. New York City.

GC: You will have before you the body of [900], of 60 West 68th Street, New York City, his mind, and the reading [900-64] of April 28, 1925, in the afternoon, and you will continue with the answering of the following questions, as I ask them, regarding these, in such a manner understandable to the mind of [900].

EC: Yes, we have the mind and the information as given in reading. We have had this before, you see. Ready for questions.

(Q) Dream regarding dark ball—earth and coming and going therefrom. What in the way and manner of the Entity prevented the body from gaining a clearer understanding of this vision? Correlate this vision with the study this entity is making of the book "Tertium Organum." [4/21/25 He referred Miss [2717] for a Life Reading, saying that she introduced him to the book "Tertium Organum" by Ouspensky: "All along I have been trying to understand this phase of your criticism of my manuscript (based on [3744] series) . . . [See 900-59, etc.] Now, why did she just show me this book?"]

(A) To give the full and complete relation and co-relation [correlation] of this, with the information and theses as given in book, would be to give a full synopsis of the information and the co-relation of impressions as given on the mind and body of [900]. The difficulty in obtaining the full impression and bringing same again to consciousness was and is the lack of being in that position to digest all as given in book, for the various sketches as have impressed the mental forces of the body, [900], are those that are nearer co-related with information as has been gained through psychic forces. As the book is the theories of Ouspensky on the psychic force manifested in the material world, then the co-relation of same becomes a matter of digesting or understanding from the various conditions, experiences of body, mind, [900], as related to that which has become in part a part and parcel, or portion of the mind, and able of digesting. Then the passing to and from the earth's plane, as seen, signifying the changes and developments that come from time to time. These and that explanation, with that as given, will be understood and able of digesting as developments come to the mental forces of the body [900], for the experience, the conditions through which this information is available, one must be in that position to feel, know and understand, without, as it were, being able to know from what sources the understanding has come.

(Q) *Explain the information or knowledge of creation, or fourth dimension life, this vision seemed to try to bring the entity.*

(A) As the illustration is given in the book of the snail's vision being that of the two-dimension, then the same to man when man, with the flexible mind of the body, becomes to that state wherein the body takes on the vision of the fourth dimension. Fourth dimension then being that condition as is reached wherein physical objects are spiritually understood, spiritual objects are physically understood, and able of experience. These become hard questions to the single track mind, or two track mind, but to the full rounded out individual become understandable conditions, to the mental processes of the well rounded mind. In this condition then does the individual reach its abilities of development in the planes as experienced in the advances from the earth's plane, coming then in that position of being able to have height, breadth, depth, thickness, and with all without space.

(Q) Vision of my grandmother in distress. Did this vision imply that the Entity had in some manner of study or otherwise caused distress to the Spiritual Forces of the Grandmother? How and why?

(A) Rather to the spiritual forces of the entity, [900], for the spiritual forces only give manifestation to that plane in which the same plane may be manifested. Rather that awakening in the mental forces, of the extenuation as it was of the fourth dimension in the physical plane, and as the body, [900] awakens, and does awaken to the elements of such conditions, the attractions become in such a nature as the physical conditions may be made manifest in the life and mind of the entity, for as is seen in how that the forces as is manifested to the entity in the spiritual guide, in father, may be again through certain laws made manifest in the physical world, so the same conditions relating to all that come under the trend of the superconscious forces of the individual. Hence, as we see in that study as is given from Confuscius [Confucius] in the spiritual law of the ancestor may be made manifest in the spiritual environment and the physical forces of the generations as they pass, so as in this vision the entity gains the insight into that which brings the depression to the spiritual forces of the physical beings, the spiritual entities.

(Q) Were the Spirit Forces or mental forces of the Spirit Entity seen in this vision making an effort to send some message to the body [900]?

(A) This is given in that just given. The spiritual force as is given here is merely the manifestation, as has been outlined, in how the change is made.

(Q) The words she said were: "You do not want me to live. Your mother doesn't want me to live." What thought or message do these words mean to imply?

(A) That there are conditions that are felt in the material world that would make under existing physical conditions detrimental forces in the body, yet the spiritual forces and environs seek to have the opportunity, under the trail as it were of existent conditions, the ability to manifest again in the material forces. These are well understood by the mind of [900].

(Q) The body [900] has received guidance from his Spiritual Guide, his Father. May he also receive guidance or communication with other Spirit Entities, such as that of his Grandmother?

(A) May receive from all whom the entity would seek guidance, when placing self in that position wherein he may gain access to that knowledge that may be implied, given or meted out from those sources.

(Q) *To what does the still small voice answer "All's Well."? Does this refer to the Spiritual Entity or to the body [900]?*

(A) To the spiritual entity that must answer within to the physical entity, [900], for the entity must wake to the realization that "the spirit beareth witness with my spirit" and the answer comes from within, and must ever come from within. Not in the thunder, not in the whirlwind, not in the storm, nor any of the mighty ravings, as it were, of nature, whether of the material forces or of the mental ravings that may shadow or be over shadowed, but ever the still small voice that answers to self, as was given.

(Q) *As is before you, the mind of [900] now understands a little better the process and means of thought communications between a spiritual Entity and an Entity on earth's plane. Explain this further in the light of the third and fourth dimension. Is every thought—say in prayer, for example, directed to or of a loved one who has passed from earth's plane by the body [900] received and understood by that Entity in the Spirit plane?*

(A) This must not be answered from here, for these reach to the realms of the superconscious forces, and each individual awakens to these developments in their individual self and should not be hampered, tied, wedged in by the thoughts and expressions of those through a material force.

(Q) *To What extent does a fourth and fifth dimension Entity guide, control, or influence affairs of the earth?*

(A) Just as much as the individual will allow same, depending upon the individual having reached the plane wherein they may attain, gain or see, understand the plane wherein such an entity having reached that plane may communicate, give force, give enlightenment, give understanding to the one of a lower dimension, for as has been given, hard for one of one faith to understand the feelings, the intent, of one of another faith, for while each intent may be in the manner to the best of their knowledge and belief, it does not affect the real status of conditions as they really exist in the various spheres, save as their co-relation [they have correlation?] have one with the other.

(Q) *Dream of Market will rally for 3 days. As given, Market rallied for 3 days, but continued to rally—to group in constructive bull market fashion. Explain this in correlation to this dream of just "3 days."*

(A) In the "3 days" we have the rallying from individual sources. After three days the general trend of all. As would be illustrated in this: We have individual commodities, individual stocks, rallying in the period, with the general trend after three days. Hence the upward trend for three days before the general trend begins.

(Q) *Conclusion—The entity [900] as you see before you, is struggling to gain the knowledge of the Universal Forces and to properly apply that knowledge. Tell the Entity how he may better act to tread in that righteous path that will bring to him, the Entity, the wisdom he seeks. The entity now alludes to the definite in his present life.*

(A) In the definite manner, keep in that way as has been set, for as has been given, there be no individual conditions to debar from the thought or action, save in the intent and purpose, and the entity only needs to keep in that straight and narrow way as the entity has set for self. There be only those specifics of knowing to make self right, not crowd same on other individuals, for "By their fruits ye shall know them."

(Q) *The Entity, [900], for example feels he understands and can explain many teachings and parables given in the Bible, which were given by Jesus. However, many who claim to follow Jesus wave his interpretations aside as ridiculous or claim he is giving a Jewish interpretation. Is the Entity properly interpreting the New Testament, which he is now studying, or are his critics correct in their criticism? As an example, the difference in opinion between the Entity [900] and [2717] on divorce as regards: "He who puts aside his wife, save for fornication, commits adultery." This question relates to the last line of the reading as given: "If thou love me, keep my commandments, for I go unto the Father and I dwell in Him and He in me." Those commandments to-day are subject to various and all sorts of interpretations. For this reason this question is asked.*

(A) The interpretations and the understandings as have [been] and are given of the teachings of Jesus are in that way and manner acceptable unto the mind of [900]. Hence they become to the individual the law, for so far as the individual makes those teachings one in life, manner and way of living, they become a part of the individual. The criticism may be from the standpoint of another condition, for each entity stands in that position as it has attained through environment, teaching and application in its individual life. In the special question as given, these stand in the same manner as is carried farther in the teachings of the Master, in that as has been given, and the law of the land wherein these are exercised and understood become the manner and light in which the individual understands same. Hence the individual interpretation of same may be taken advantage of through the civil conditions. Hence civil laws, spiritual law, material law, are of an entire different condition, for the individual only gains that to which it has developed. Then the interpretation as given by the body, [900], to the body law. To others as they view same.

We are through for the present.

3

●

Cayce's Series on the Sixth Sense

Text of Reading 5754-1

This psychic reading given by Edgar Cayce at his home on Arctic Crescent, Virginia Beach, Va., this 14th day of July, 1932, in accordance with request made by Hugh Lynn Cayce and those present.

PRESENT

Edgar Cayce; Gertrude Cayce, Conductor; Gladys Davis, Steno. Mildred Davis, Edgar Evans Cayce, and Polly the parrot. (Also canary in cage.)

Time of Reading 4:30 P.M.

GC: You will please outline clearly and comprehensively the material which should be presented to the general public in explaining just what occurs in the conscious, subconscious and spiritual forces of an entity while in the state known as sleep. Please answer the questions which will be asked regarding this:

EC: Yes. While there has been a great deal written and spoken regarding experiences of individuals in that state called sleep, there has only recently been the attempt to control or form any definite idea of what produces conditions in the unconscious, subconscious, or sub-liminal or subnormal mind, by attempts to produce a character—or to determine that which produces the character—of dream as had by an individual or entity. Such experiments may determine for some minds questions respecting the claim of some psychiatrist or psycho-analyst and through such experiments refute or determine the value of such in the study of certain character of mental disturbances in individuals; yet little of this may be called true analysis of what happens to the body, either physical, mental, subconscious or spiritual, when it loses itself in such repose. To be sure, there are certain definite conditions that take place respecting the physical, the conscious, and the subconscious, as well as spiritual forces of a body.

So, in analyzing such a state for a comprehensive understanding, all things pertaining to these various factors must be considered.

First, we would say, sleep is a shadow of, that intermission in earth's experiences of, that state called death; for the physical consciousness becomes unaware of existent conditions, save as are determined by the attributes of the physical that partake of the attributes of the imagina-tive or the subconscious and unconscious forces of that same body; that is, in a normal sleep (physical standpoint we are reasoning now) the *senses* are on guard, as it were, so that the auditory forces are those that are the more sensitive.

The auditory sense being of the attributes or senses that are more universal in aspect, when matter in its evolution has become aware of itself being capable of taking from that about itself to sustain itself in its present state. That is as of the lowest to the highest of animate objects or beings. From the lowest of evolution to the highest, or to man.

So, then, we find that there are left what is ordinarily known as four other attributes that are acting independently and coordinatingly in *awareness* for a physical body to be conscious. These, in the state of sleep or repose, or rest, or exhaustion, or induced by any influence from the outside, have become *unaware* of that which is taking place about the object so resting.

Then, there is the effect that is had upon the body as to what be-comes, then, more aware to those attributes of the body that are not aware of that existent about them, or it. The organs that are of that portion known as the inactive, or not necessary for conscious movement, keep right on with their functioning—as the pulsations, the heart beat, the assimilating and excretory system, keep right on functioning; yet there are periods during such a rest when even the heart, the circulation, may be said to be at rest. What, then, *is* that that is not in action during such period? That known as the sense of perception as related to the physical brain. Hence it may be truly said, by the analogy of that given, that the auditory sense is sub-divided, and there is the act of hearing by feeling, the act of hearing by the sense of smell, the act of hearing by *all* the senses that are independent of the brain centers themselves, but are rather of the lymph centers—or throughout the entire sympathetic system is such an accord as to be *more* aware, *more* acute, even though the body-physical and brain-physical *is* at repose, or *unaware.*

Of what, then, does this sixth sense partake, that has to do so much with the entity's activities by those actions that may be brought about by that passing within the sense *range* of an entity when in repose, that may be called—in their various considerations or phases—experiences of *something* within that entity, as a dream—that may be either in toto to that which is to happen, is happening, or may be only presented in some form that is emblematical—to the body or those that would interpret such.

These, then—or this, then—the sixth sense, as it may be termed for consideration here, partakes of the *accompanying* entity that is ever on guard before the throne of the Creator itself, and is that that may be trained or submerged, or left to its *own* initiative until it makes either war *with* the self in some manner of expression—which must show itself in a material world as in dis-ease, or disease, or temper, or that we call the blues, or the grouches, or any form that may receive either in the waking state or in the sleep state, that has *enabled* the brain in its activity to become so changed or altered as to respond much in the manner as does a string tuned that vibrates to certain sound in the manner in which it is strung or played upon.

Then we find, this sense that governs such is that as may be known as the other self of the entity, or individual. Hence we find there must be some definite line that may be taken by that other self, and much that then has been accorded—or recorded—as to that which may produce certain given effects in the minds or bodies (not the minds, to be sure, for its active forces are upon that outside of that in which the mind, as ordinarily known, or the brain centers themselves, functions), but—as may be seen by all such experimentation, these may be produced—the same effect—upon the same individual, but they do not produce the same effect upon a different individual in the same environment or under the same circumstance. Then, this should lead one to know, to understand, that there is a *definite* connection between that we have chosen to term the sixth sense, or acting through the auditory forces of the body–physical, and the other self within self.

In purely physical, we find in sleep the body is *relaxed*—and there is little or no tautness within same, and those activities that function through the organs that are under the supervision of the sub–conscious or unconscious self, through the involuntary activities of an organism that has been set in motion by that impulse it has received from its first germ cell force, and its activity by the union *of* those forces that have been impelled or acted upon by that it has fed upon in all its efforts and activities that come, then it may be seen that these may be shown by due consideration—that the same body fed upon *meats*, and for a period—then the same body fed upon only herbs and fruits—would *not* have the same character or activity of the other self in its relationship to that as would be experienced by the other self in its activity through that called the dream self.

We are through for the moment—present.

Text of Reading 5754-2

This psychic reading given by Edgar Cayce at his home on Arctic Crescent, Virginia Beach, Va., this 15th day of July, 1932, in accordance with request made by those present.

PRESENT

Edgar Cayce; Gertrude Cayce, Conductor; Gladys Davis, Steno. Mildred Davis.

READING

Time of Reading 11:30 A.M.

EC: Now, with that as has just been given, that there is an active force within each individual that functions in the manner of a sense when the body–physical is in sleep, repose or rest, we would then outline as to what are the functions of this we have chosen to call a sixth sense.

What relation does it bear with the normal physical recognized five senses of a physical–aware body? If these are active, what relation do they bear to this sixth sense?

Many words have been used in attempting to describe what the spiritual entity of a body is, and what relations this spirit or soul bears with or to the active forces within a physical normal body. Some have chosen to call this the cosmic body, and the cosmic body as a sense in the universal consciousness, or that portion of same that is a part of, or that body with which the individual, or man, is clothed in his advent into the material plane.

These are correct in many respects, yet by their very classification, or by calling them by names to designate their faculties or functionings, have been limited in many respects.

But what relation has this sixth sense (as has been termed in this presented) with this *soul* body, this cosmic consciousness? What relation has it with the faculties and functionings of the normal physical mind? Which must be trained? The sixth sense? or must the body be trained in its other functionings to the dictates of the sixth sense?

In that as presented, we find this has been termed, that this ability or this functioning—that is so active when physical consciousness is laid aside—or, as has been termed by some poet, when the body rests in the arms of Morpheus—is nearer possibly to that as may be understandable by or to many; for, as given, this activity—as is seen—of a mind, or an attribute of the mind in physical activity—*leaves* a *definite* impression. Upon what? The mental activities of the body, or upon the subconscious portion of the body (which, it has been termed that, it never forgets), upon the spiritual essence of the body, or upon the soul itself? These are questions, not statements!

In understanding, then, let's present illustrations as a pattern, that there may be comprehension of that which is being presented:

The activity, or this sixth sense activity, is the activating power or force of the other self. What other self? That which has been builded by the entity or body, or soul, through its experiences as a whole in the material and cosmic world, see? or is as a faculty of the soul-body itself. Hence, as the illustration given, does the subconscious make aware to this active force when the body is at rest, or this sixth sense, some action on the part of self or another that is in disagreement with that which has been builded by that other self, then *this* is the warring of conditions or emotions within an individual. Hence we may find that an individual may from sorrow *sleep* and wake with a feeling of elation. What has taken place? We possibly may then understand what we are speaking of. There has been, and ever when the physical consciousness is at rest, the other self communes with the *soul* of the body, see? or it goes *out* into that realm of experience in the relationships of all experiences of that entity that may have been throughout the *eons* of time, or in correlating *with* that as it, that entity, *has* accepted as its criterion or standard of judgments, or justice, within its sphere of activity.

Hence through such an association in sleep there may have come that peace, that understanding, that is accorded by that which has been correlated through that passage of the selves of a body in sleep. Hence we find the more spiritual-minded individuals are the more easily pacified, at peace, harmony, in normal active state as well as in sleep. Why? They have set before themselves (Now we are speaking of one individual!) that that *is* a criterion that may be wholly relied upon, for that from which an entity or soul sprang is its *concept*, its awareness of, the divine or creative forces within their experience. Hence they that have named the Name of the Son have put their trust in Him. He their standard, their model, their hope, their activity. Hence we see how that the action through such sleep, or such quieting as to enter the silence— What do we mean by entering the silence? Entering the presence of that which *is* the criterion of the selves of an entity!

On the other hand oft we find one may retire with a feeling of elation, or peace, and awaken with a feeling of depression, of aloofness, of being alone, of being without hope, or of fear entering, and the *body-physical* awakes with that depression that manifests itself as of low spirits, as is termed, or of coldness, gooseflesh over the body, in expressions of the forces. What has taken place? A comparison in that "arms of

Morpheus", in that silence, in that relationship of the physical self being unawares of those comparisons between the soul and its experiences of that period with the experiences of itself throughout the ages, and the experience may not have been remembered as a dream—but it lives *on*—and on, and must find its expression in the relationships of all it has experienced in whatever sphere of activity it may have found itself. Hence we find oft individual circumstances of where a spiritual-minded individual in the material plane (that is, to outward appearances of individuals so viewing same) suffering oft under pain, sickness, sorrow, and the like. What takes place? The experiences of the soul are meeting that which it has merited, for the clarification for the associations of itself with that whatever has been set as its ideal. If one has set self in array against that of love as manifested by the Creator, in its activity brought into material plane, then there *must* be a continual—continual—*warring* of those elements. By the comparison we may find, then, how it was that, that energy of creation manifested in the Son—by the activities of the Son in the material plane, could say "He sleeps", while to the outward eye it was death; for He *was*—and *is*—and ever will be—Life and Death in one; for as we find ourselves *in* His presence, that we have builded in the soul makes for that condemnation or that pleasing of the presence of that in His presence. So, my son, let thine lights be in Him, for these are the *manners* through which all may come to an understanding of the activities; for, as was given, "I was in the Spirit on the Lord's day." "I was caught up to the seventh heaven. Whether I was in the body or out of the body I cannot tell." What was taking place? The subjugation of the physical attributes in accord and attune with its infinite force as set as its ideal brought to that soul, "Well done, thou good and faithful servant, enter into the joys of thy Lord." "He that would be the greatest among you—" Not as the Gentiles, not as the heathen, not as the scribes or Pharisees, but "He that would be the greatest will be the *servant* of all."

What, then, has this to do—you ask—with the subject of sleep? Sleep— that period when the soul takes stock of that it has acted upon during one rest period to another, making or drawing—as it were—the comparisons that make for Life itself in its *essence*, as for harmony, peace, joy, love, long-suffering, patience, brotherly love, kindness—these are the fruits of the Spirit. Hate, harsh words, unkind thoughts, oppressions and the like, these are the fruits of the evil forces, or Satan and the soul either abhors that it has passed, or enters into the joy of its Lord. Hence we see the activities of same. This an *essence* of that which is intuitive in the active forces. Why should this be so in one portion, or one part of a body, rather than another? How received woman her awareness? Through the sleep of the man! Hence *intuition* is an attribute of that made aware through the suppression of those forces from that from which it sprang, yet endowed *with* all of those abilities and forces of its Maker that made for same its activity in an *aware* world, or—if we choose to term it such—a three dimensional world, a *material* world, where its beings must see a materialization to become aware of its existence in that plane; yet all are aware that the essence of Life itself as the air that is breathed—carries those elements that are not aware consciously of any existence to the body, yet the body subsists, lives upon such. In sleep all things become possible, as one finds self flying through space, lifting, or being chased, or what not, by those very things that make for a comparison of that which has been builded by the very soul of the body itself.

What, then, is the sixth sense? Not the soul, not the conscious mind, not the subconscious mind, not intuition alone, not any of those cosmic forces—but the very force or activity of the soul in its experience through *whatever* has been the experience of that soul itself. See? The same as we would say, is the mind of the body the body? No! Is the sixth sense, then, the soul? No! No more than the mind is the body! for the soul is the *body* of, or the spiritual essence of, an entity manifested in this material plane.

We are through for the present.

Text of Reading 5754-3

This psychic reading given by Edgar Cayce at his home on Arctic Crescent, Va. Beach, Va. this 15th day of July, 1932, in accordance with request made by those present.

PRESENT

Edgar Cayce; Gertrude Cayce, Conductor; Gladys Davis, Steno. Mildred Davis.

READING

Time of Reading 4:45 P.M.

EC: Yes, we have that which has been given here. Now, as we have that condition that exists with the body and this functioning, or this sense, or this ability of sleep and sense, or a sixth sense, just what, how, may this knowledge be used to advantage for an individual's development towards that it would attain?

As to how it may be used, then, depends upon what is the ideal of that individual; for, as has been so well pointed out in Holy Writ, if the ideal of the individual is lost, then the abilities for that faculty or that sense of an individual to contact the spiritual forces are gradually lost, or barriers are built that prevent this from being a sensing of the nearness of an individual to a spiritual development.

As to those who are nearer the spiritual realm, their visions, dreams, and the like, are more often—and are more often retained by the individual; for, as is seen as a first law, it is self-preservation. Then self rarely desires to condemn self, save when the selves are warring one with another, as are the elements within a body when eating of that which produces what is termed a nightmare—they are warring with the senses of the body, and partake either of those things that make afraid, or produce visions of the nature as partaking of the elements that are taken within the system, and active within same itself. These may be given as examples of what it is all about.

Then, how may this be used to develop a body in its relationship to the material, the mental, and the spiritual forces?

Whether the body desires or not, in sleep the consciousness physically is laid aside. As to what will be that it will seek, depends upon what has been builded as that it would associate itself with, physically, mentally, spiritually, and the closer the association in the mental mind in the physical forces, in the physical attributes, are with spiritual elements, then—as has been seen by even those attempting to produce a certain character of vision or dream—these follow much in that; for another law that is universal becomes active! Like begets like! That which is sown in honor is reaped in glory. That which is sown in corruption cannot be reaped in glory; and the likings are associations that are the companions of that which has been builded; for such experiences as dreams, visions and the like, are but the *activities* in the unseen world of the real self of an entity.

Ready for questions.

(Q) *How may one train the sixth sense?*

(A) This has just been given; that which is constantly associated in the mental visioning in the imaginative forces, that which is constantly associated with the senses of the body, that will it develop toward. What is that which is and may be sought? When under stress *many* an individual—There are *no* individuals who haven't at *some time* been warned as respecting that that may arise in their daily or physical experience! Have they heeded? Do they heed to that as may be given as advice? No! It must be experienced!

(Q) *How may one be constantly guided by the accompanying entity on guard at the Throne?*

(A) It is there! It's as to whether they desire or not! It doesn't leave but is the active force? As to its ability to *sense* the variations in the experiences that are seen, is as has been given in the illustration—"As to whether in the body or out of the body, I cannot tell." Hence this sense is that ability of the entity to associate its physical, mental or spiritual self to that realm that it, the entity, or the mind of the soul, seeks for its association during such periods—see? This might confuse some, for—as has been given—the subconscious and the abnormal, or the unconscious conscious, is the mind of the soul; that is, the sense that this is used, as being that subconscious or subliminal self that is on guard ever with the Throne itself; for has it not been said, "He has given his angels charge concerning thee, lest at any time thou dashest thy foot against a stone?" Have you heeded? Then He is near. Have you disregarded? He has withdrawn to thine own self, see? That self that has been builded, that that is as the companion, that must be presented—that *is* presented—*is* before the Throne itself! *consciousness*—[physical] consciousness—see—man seeks this for his *own* diversion. In the sleep [the soul] seeks the *real* diversion, or the *real* activity of self.

(Q) *What governs the experiences of the astral body while in the fourth dimensional plane during sleep?*

(A) This is, as has been given, that upon which it has fed. That which it has builded; that which it seeks; that which the mental mind, the subconscious mind, the subliminal mind, *seeks!* That governs. Then we come to an understanding of that, "He that would find must seek." In the physical or material this we understand. That is a pattern of the subliminal or the spiritual self.

(Q) What state or trend of development is indicated if an individual does not remember dreams?

(A) The negligence of its associations, both physical, mental and spiritual. Indicates a very negligible personage!

(Q) Does one dream continually but simply fail to remember consciously?

(A) Continues an association or withdraws from that which *is* its right, or its ability to associate! There is no difference in the unseen world to that that is visible, save in the unseen so much greater expanse or space may be covered! Does one always desire to associate itself with others? Do individuals always seek companionship in this or that period of their experiences in each day? Do they withdraw themselves from? That desire lies or carries on! See? It's a *natural* experience! It's *not* an unnatural! Don't seek for unnatural or supernatural! It is the natural—it is nature—it is God's activity! His associations with man. His *desire* to make for man a way for an understanding! Is there seen or understood fully that illustration that was given of the Son of man, that while those in the ship were afraid because of the elements the Master of the sea, of the elements, slept? What associations may there have been with that sleep? Was it a natural withdrawing? yet when spoken to, the sea and the winds obeyed His voice. Thou may do even as He, wilt thou make thineself aware—whether that awareness through the ability of those forces within self to communicate with, understand, those elements of the spiritual life *in* the conscious and unconscious, these be one!

(Q) Is it possible for a conscious mind to dream while the astral or spirit body is absent?

(A) There may be dreams—(This is a division here) A conscious mind, while the body is absent, is as one's ability to divide self and do two things at once, as is seen by the activities of the mental mind.

The ability to read music and play is using different faculties of the same mind. Different portions of the same consciousness. Then, for one faculty to function while another is functioning in a different direction is not only possible but probable, dependent upon the ability of the individual to concentrate, or to centralize in their various places those functionings that are manifest of the spiritual forces in the material plane. *Beautiful*, isn't it?

(Q) *What connection is there between the physical or conscious mind and the spiritual body during sleep or during an astral experience?*

(A) It's as has been given, that *sensing!* With what? That separate sense, or the ability of sleep, that makes for acuteness with those forces in the physical being that are manifest in everything animate. As the unfolding of the rose, the quickening in the womb, of the grain as it buds forth, the awakening in all nature of that which has been set by the divine forces, to make the awareness of its presence in *matter*, or material things.

We are through for the present.

4

●

Cayce's Guidance for Developing Psychic Ability

Text of Reading 137-3 M 26

This psychic reading given by Edgar Cayce at 60 West 68th Street, New York city, New York, this 13th day of October, 1924, in accordance with request made by self—[137].

PRESENT

Edgar Cayce; Morton H. Blumenthal, Conductor; (?), Steno. [137], David E. Kahn, and others (?).

READING

Time of Reading Unknown.

MHB: You are going to sleep in a quiet, restful manner and you will hear me as I speak to you and ask the questions slowly and distinctly.

You have before you the body of [137]. You will answer the questions slowly and distinctly. You have in place the body of [137].

EC: Yes, we have the body here. We have had this before, you see.

(Q) In a previous reading, you told this body that he himself was a psychic. You will tell him how he will develop this psychic ability.

(A) As has been given, we have in the material world the two known and accepted conditions. The body and the material world. The projection from the body or from a material world is of that unknown element called psychic. See?

We have those forces in the mental, or soul forces that with the spirit inside of entity shall manifest itself, that the phenomena or psychic forces become perceptible to the individual entity. The training, the knowledge, the understanding of such forces may be developed in this body through certain lines that are as sure conditions. As given, in this manner and form, may same be developed, giving a certain given period to concentrate his body physically, mentally, entering the silence. Come apart from the outside world, the thoughts, perceptions of the outside forces, alone entering into the silence for 15 to 20 minutes each day at first. See?

Giving the body the time, the spirit forces of such entity aside, and then enter into the magic silence and instantly force those projections from the manifested forces of the world, of material, of psychic, those conditions that will make to the individual the understanding, the knowledge of the psychic forces as are in the world, and that may be made manifested in this individual entity [137]. For with each entering in through concentrations, with awakening of that entity forces quick arising conditions that arise through such a condition as has manifested through psychic forces. The use of such forces in a material world is the greater gift of any entity. This body would understand from this conception the perception of such knowledge and the use of same.

In this manner may the body fully understand such conditions. Well that these be guided by that injunction as will be found in the last verse of Deuteronomy 29, and the whole chapter of 30.

(Q) *Where shall this body take this solitude, when concentrating?*

(A) Any place the body may choose, being alone, and in the same place each day.

(Q) *Is any such hour suggested for this concentration?*

(A) No, any hour, only using the same hour each day, entering with the supplication to the Giver of all good and perfect gifts.

(Q) *How can this body learn to concentrate as suggested?*

(A) This is the special gift of this entity. Through the supplications set aside the cares, the thoughts, of the outside world and study those conditions that mind enters at such concentrations, at times and certain times that come through the mental forces of the body.

(Q) After this has been developed, how can the psychic power of this body be used?

(A) In developing same in the lives of others, not to become as one that would be evil-spoken of, but that that gives the other living possession of the holy one within the lives of each and every individual that will awaken to the indwelling of Him who gives life to all.

(Q) Is it pre-ordained that this body should have the use of this power?

(A) Pre-ordained in that entity, as gained through this mode and manner of conducting this will, with that of the Divine Spirit as is given in injunction "My spirit beareth witness with your spirit, whether ye be the sons of God or not." In this entity this has been kept, and the body keeps the living way within itself and presents the body, soul and spirit, holy and acceptable unto Him, which is a reasonable service.

(Q) How long will it be necessary for the body to go into these solitudes before this body will have the use of a psychic power?

(A) Twenty to thirty days.

(Q) After these periods of concentration, what should be done to develop the body's psychic power?

(A) For those particular injunctions that come to the individual self in such moments, same may be used in the material and in the psychic way, so long as it is done in an unselfish manner.

(Q) Should this body read any literature on the subject of the psychic? If so, what literature?

(A) Those as indicated we find the best study of psychic literature given.

(Q) How can this body study himself?

(A) Study this injunction as given in the manner and way given.

(Q) Will the development of this psychic force imprison this body as far as he personally is concerned?

(A) It improves the body materially, mentally, physically, spiritually and financially.

(Q) Would you suggest anything further to this body?

(A) We are through for the present.

Text of Reading 137-5 M 26

This psychic reading given by Edgar Cayce at his office, 322 Grafton Avenue, Dayton, Ohio, this 2nd day of November,

1924, in accordance with request made by his brother, [900].

PRESENT

Edgar Cayce; Mrs. Cayce, Conductor; Gladys Davis, Steno.
Archie Adlman, Hugh Lynn Cayce, and [900].

READING

Time of Reading 10:00 P.M. Dayton Time. New York City, N.Y.

GC: Now you have before you [137], who was at his apartment, . . .
Street, New York, on the fourth floor, at nine A.M. November 2, 1924.
You will give a spiritual and mental reading, giving us the names of his
spiritual guides. Also tell us if he is carrying out the suggestions properly to develop the psychic forces, or what he may do to better develop
these forces. You will also answer any questions I might ask you relative
to these.

EC: Yes, we have the body here. We have had this before, you see,
with the mental and the spiritual forces in and with this body or entity.

In this we find the exceptional forces manifested in this entity
through the mental and the spiritual forces, and the body prepares the
mental well for the soul development of the entity.

We would not give change for the mental or spiritual development
for this entity; only be thou faithful unto the end.

As to the guides in this entity, we find the exemplification of the
forces innate in the developments in earth plane guiding the present
entity's mental forces, through the spiritual nature as developed upon
the earth plane. Hence the ability of the entity to develop the psychic
forces to the consciousness of the conscious and subconscious minds of
the entity, for the psychic forces are the projection of soul development
in the earth plane.

The manner in which the body goes about these developments at
this time is very good, only the body should not attempt to consciously
prevent the conscious losing itself in sleep or slumber, for through this
we will find the first action of the psychic making the physical manifestation to the conscious mind, and with those impressions gained in
such condition use those at once, and the conscious will find the developing of the psychic or latent forces in the present earth plane and may

be able to use those manifestations for the development of self and of others. This is the correct way to develop the forces, [137].

(Q) Has the body not definite guides in spirit sphere?

(A) Development sufficient, as given, that the entity's guide the innermost conditions in the physical plane. Hence the ability of manifesting through the psychic forces, as given.

(Q) How will psychic manifest in the physical?

(A) First through the lapse of consciousness, which the body should not warn or fight against when entering the silence, and through such lapses will the first development show. There have been two already, only one acted upon. Act immediately.

(Q) What were these two?

(A) One came only as names. Again came as actions in the daily labors.

(Q) Will [137] be able to give psychic readings like Edgar Cayce?

(A) The development is beyond those conditions as given by Edgar Cayce, for they will become conscious conditions to be acted upon by the conscious mind; that is, the impressions received in the Borderland, and be able to bring same to consciousness from the physical standpoint.

(Q) What was the name that came to him in this first?

(A) He has that. He acted upon it.

(Q) What was the second?

(A) Second not acted upon. Had to do with stocks.

(Q) Has he already acquired these psychic powers?

(A) Developing them. Do not go against those conditions, would the development be to the better. Act upon but do not take advantage of others, using same rather to assist and develop the latent forces in entities upon whom the forces direct the entity's endeavors.

(Q) How may he use this psychic power to assist in the work of Edgar Cayce?

(A) By entering into these conditions, with the questions necessary, before any group who may develop the powers and forces. They will work well together, one beyond or above the other, you see.

Text of Reading 440-8 M 23
(Elec. Engr. Student, Christian)

This psychic reading given by Edgar Cayce at his home on Arctic Crescent, Virginia Beach, Va., this 21st day of December, 1933, in accordance with request made by self—Mr. [440], Active Member of the Ass'n for Research & Enlightenment, Inc.

PRESENT

Edgar Cayce; Gertrude Cayce, Conductor; Gladys Davis, Steno. Mr. [440], Mildred Davis, L. B. and Hugh Lynn Cayce.

READING

Time of Reading 5:05 to 5:45 P.M. Eastern Standard Time. New York City.

(Entity and soul–mind. You will give complete guidance for this entity in developing and manifesting correctly his psychic faculties in this present life. Ans. Ques.) (Before concluding this reading in the usual manner by saying "We are through," you will say, "We are ready for the final request from this entity.")

EC: Yes, we have the entity and the soul–mind, [440], present in this room.

In giving that which may be the better or the correct manner of developing the soul faculties, or the psychic forces of the entity, this may be given better in the way and manner as a diet might be outlined for a physical body.

That from experience to experience there are found those things that do not answer at the time for the better expression or manifesting of the psychic and soul forces of a body, is the experience of each soul as it presses onward to the mark of the higher calling that is set in the ideal chosen by an entity to be guided by, or to parallel self's development with, or self's development towards.

But, as understood—or should be by each soul, the development must be *self*-development, *soul* development.

That the psychic faculties of a soul or entity are the manners through which manifestations may come from the outside and from within, is the experience of most individuals in their development; though they may call such manifestations by many names, that are seen or given under various lines of thought or various manners of development. Yet these expressions or manifestations are, as we would give, of the soul or the psychic faculties of the soul, or soul or spirit world.

Then, in the preparation for this entity, [440], as given, the body, the mind, the soul, is well balanced for a development. There are those experiences in the development that would tend to make for either very high development or for the turning of the development into destructive forces; not intentionally at all times, but that *tendency* for extravagance of self, as it were, in that direction. This, then, is rather as the warning:

First, as indicated, *find self.* Find what is self's ideal. And as to how high that ideal is. Does it consist of or pertains to materiality, or spirituality? Does it bespeak of self-development or selfless development for the glory of the ideal? And be sure that the ideal is rather of the spiritual. And this may become, as given, the first psychic experience of self's own inner soul, or self's own guide—as may be chosen. And do not be satisfied with a guide other than from the Throne of Grace itself! And when the self is being taught, seek a teacher. When self needs exhortation, then seek an exhorter. When self is desiring or seeking those channels that pertain to the material, or the application of material things, that spiritual lessons or spiritual truths may be brought, then *seek* such a source, such a channel for the *creative* influences. And who better may be such a guide than the Creator *of* the universe? For, He has given that "If ye will seek me ye may find me" and "I will not leave thee comfortless" but if ye are righteous in purpose, in intent, in desire, "I will bring *all things* to thine remembrance" that are needs be for thy soul, thine mind, thine body, development.

This is a promise from Him, who is able to fulfill that which has been promised to every soul that seeks His face, His ways.

Then, speak oft with thy Maker. And let thine meditation be:

Lord, use Thou me in that way, in that manner, that I—as Thy son, thy servant— may be of the greater service to my fellow man. And may I know His biddings, Father, as Thou hast promised that if we would hear Him that we ask in His name may be ours. I claim that relationship, Father, and I seek Thy guidance day by day!

And, as the light comes, as the feelings of the understandings come—never by chance, but in His ways doth He bring to pass that way, that channel, those individuals *through* whom self may make for *soul's* development—through those things that may come to thee, do ye walk in the Way.

This, then, is the manner for self to develop, for self to know, for self to understand.

Naturally, the question arises within self, how shall I know?

In what manner will it be given me to know who is giving the information, who is speaking?

As outlined, first the answer is within self's own mental self, as to whatever is being sought.

Then in the meditation of that given in outline as a diet for the soul body, for the psychic faculties, the answer will be in the spirit. And each time, each experience when there is being sought for self as to What manner of activity or what manner or course is the right way to pursue, may it be given what manner or could thee in the same way and manner.

If the approach is through some associate, some friend, some brother that is acting in the capacity as a sign, as a guide post along the way of life, then know that thou hast been guided to that way—and ye yourself must walk that road; and that ye may not walk alone—rather with His guiding hand will the way be shown, will the way be made plain in thine endeavors.

Keep self out of the way. Stumble not over the pitfalls that arise from self's anxiety, self's indulgences or self's expression of aggrandized interests—but let thy ways be His ways. Then ye shall know the truth and the truth shall make you free.

Ready for questions.

(Q) *Would a development of automatic writing establish a better contact with my Maker?*

(A) For this body we would not give automatic writing as the channel. Rather the intuitional, or the meditation and then writing—*knowing* what is being written, if it's chosen to be inscribed in ink.

(Q) *Has entity reached a point in his development where he contacts or may contact the White Brotherhood?*

(A) The brother of brothers, the Christ!

(Q) Explain and describe the activity of this entity in the spiritual realm as indicated in his Life Reading as follows: "For, as from the spiritual plane through which the entity has been active—"

(A) This has been given, as to how that from plane to plane *between* the earth's appearances there was the cleansing of self, that has made for a balancing in the three definite positions given in the present. A balancing in the body, the mind, the soul.

Hence, in the interim through those experiences when the soul in the planetary environ learned its lesson to apply same.

Hence *this* entity, *this* soul's development and manifestation must be the more in materiality. Hence the warnings as respecting same, and the *desire* that should be as a *consuming* desire to not be satisfied with other than that as may be answered in the questions through self's approach to that Throne, as given.

Then may there *ever* be known to self as to any approach, to any channel, or any source that may supply information of any nature—*self* should know intuitively whether "I believe it," or whether it is true or whether it is worth the trouble of correcting such a brother. Hence the work, the activities, will be twofold—and not only enlightening self but opening the eyes of the blind to the pitfalls they are entering in their approach to light. See? Beautiful position! But one that demands not longfacedness but a joyousness in the service. For *who*, my brother—*who* would be thy companion in the service thou may render to thy brothers here, there? As He will guide you! But first—*first* find self. And know thy ideal. Be on speaking terms with Him.

(Q) Please explain experience which occurred at Ommen, Holland in 1928 or 1929, where the entity seemed to lose control of his body. It occurred at about 3:00 A.M.

(A) When there was being the experience of that as may be read: "Peter, Satan hath desired thee. Keep, then, the way that has been opened before thee." It, the experience then, was that there was the meeting of the ways between self and self's choice, as is and will be known as the body-mind and soul advances in the experience. That experience has been the turning point in the *seeking* for soul's understanding, and soul's attributes, from that experience.

(Q) Explain why the terrifying sensation results from lying on back and placing hands under head.

(A) An unbalancing of the forces through which, in the physical body, the psychic sources are opened. We would refer you to that which has been given as respecting same. Hence the hands should always cross the solar plexus, the *balancing* between the forces of the body when meditating or seeking for the opening of self to the unseen sources—but never open self, my friend, without surrounding self with the spirit of the Christ, that ye may ever be guarded and guided by His forces!

(Q) *Is this done in the manner indicated?*

(A) In the manner of crossing the hands over the solar plexus, either on the plexus area—the 9th dorsal—or the umbilical plexus—as indicated in the body here [Edgar Cayce] through which this information comes.

(Q) *What musical instrument am I best fitted to play?*

(A) The oboe would be the better, though if there are to be the considerations of using the instrument with self's development or attuning self to the vibrations, this—still—as we find—would be the better instrument.

(Q) *Where have I been associated with my mother [See 443-1] in the past?*

(A) As *specifically* indicated, the greater *spiritual development* in the Egyptian manifestation. The greater *material*, in the early Colonial period—or pre-Colonial period.

(Q) *Does our work lie together in this life?*

(A) Rather paralleled, and one is a check or a balance for the other. Do not interfere with each one's development at the present period, but *ever* must each be the balance one for the other.

(Q) *Please explain the connection and what will result from the association with [4947], whom I helped through Harvard last year—Engineering school.*

(A) When there were the activities in the early part of the associations in the pre-Colonial period, or in and about Pennsylvania. Look to much of those activities that will later come together to the self, in the thirty-fourth and thirty-fifth year of the life—and you'll need each other then.

(Q) *What should be my relationship to the opposite sex?*

(A) Those that are of kindred thought are, of natural intent, an aid to a soul that seeks. They that are of a different bent, and have no interest in common, are naturally those that hinder or prevent. For, they are still wily as Eve was with Adam!

(Q) *In what year is it best for marriage, or should I marry at all?*

(A) Twenty–eighth year.

(Q) *Have I known Miss [4944] before, . . . , N.Y.C.?*

(A) An association that was both good and bad. These came in those periods when the body itself was in turmoils, in the Atlantean experience.

(Q) *Can you tell me the same about [. . .] [Mrs. [465]'s daughter] . . . , N.Y.C.?*

(A) Be good for each other! One's a stimuli one for the other.

We are ready for the question.

(Q) *In concluding these readings for the present, I wish to express my sincere gratitude and appreciation for the information which has been given me. Give me your blessing, that I may use this information only for the betterment of conditions, in accordance with the will of God.*

(A) May His blessings abide with thee. May He keep thee, and bless thee, and bring thee to thine proper relationships with thine Maker, thine God, thine ideal.

We are through.

Editor's Note: The following reading was given as a kind of swap between two renowned psychics: Edgar Cayce and Eileen Garrett. Mrs. Garrett used a spirit guide to help her get information and guidance. On the day before this following reading, Mrs. Garrett and her spirit guide Uvani gave a "reading" for Edgar Cayce. The following is Edgar Cayce's reading for Mrs. Garrett. He begins with a general view of psychic ability, then focuses on her specific ability, and then responds to the changes that Mrs. Garrett and Uvani suggested for Cayce.

Text of Reading 507-1

This psychic reading given by Edgar Cayce at the home of Mr. and Mrs. Ernest W. Zentgraf, 400 St. Paul's Ave., Stapleton, S.I., N.Y., this 3rd day of February, 1934, in accordance with request made by those present—and by self, Mrs. Eileen Garrett, new Associate Member of the Ass'n for Research & Enlightenment, Inc., recommended by Mrs. T. Mitchell Hastings.

PRESENT

Edgar Cayce; Hugh Lynn Cayce, Conductor; Gladys Davis, Steno. Eileen Garrett; Margaret Naumberg; T. Mitchell Hastings; Helene, Ernest, Robert, Margret and Lilian Zentgraf; Eleanor and Adolph Ostwald.

READING

Time of Reading, 11:50 to 12:25 P.M. Eastern Standard Time. 33 West 51st Street, NYC.

HLC: Now you will have before you the soul entity now known as Eileen Garrett, present in this room. You will give at this time such information regarding her work which will be interesting and helpful in relation to our experiments today. You will answer the questions which I will ask.

EC: Yes, we have the entity, the soul entity, Eileen Garrett, here, present in this room.

As to that which may be helpful to those that seek to know that there is the continuity of life, that there is to be gained from those activities in the realm of soul forces that may act through the psychic forces in each individual soul, know that that which may be given through this entity is that which is received through the varied channels that present themselves in that atmosphere or that environ that seeks for an understanding in those fields of activity that may bring to the manifested actions of individuals those influences that may have to bear upon the lives and souls of individuals.

As to how, to whom, or from what sources these emanations or activities may take their action, depends upon first the sincerity of purpose, as to whether it is to be constructive in the experience of such seekers of whether through self there is to be the aggrandizement of power, influence or force upon and in the experience. For, as ye sow, so shall ye reap.

As there are only those influences in self that may separate the knowledge of the constructive influence in the life; so only self may find those influences through such a channel that will be to meet the needs of those things necessary in self's experience for the greater development.

Ready for questions.

(Q) Explain how this information is now being given for Mrs. Garrett, the source of this information.

(A) Being given through that which has been builded in the life and the experience of Mrs. Garrett, and taken from those records made by such activities.

(Q) What is the source of Mrs. Garrett's psychic information?

(A) A portion is from the soul development of the entity, that has made and does make for a channel through which spiritual or psychic forces may manifest in a material world; and thus giving that to which the seekers may find in their own particular field of activity. Also from those influences from without that are either in those attitudes of being teachers, instructors, directors, or those that would give to those in the material plane the better comprehension of the continuance of a mental and soul activity.

(Q) For what purpose was this power given to her?

(A) That there might be given, as it were, the opportunity for the soul to use that it had builded within self to make for a manifestation in a material world of those influences that are without and within. For, as has been given, the spirit maketh alive—and the kingdom of truth and light is within. With the abilities that are manifested through this soul entity, of subjugation of the influences from the material or carnal influences of experience, making then for self a channel through which there may come those forces or sources from the source of *all* supply. For, the Father giveth ever the increase, whether in material things, mental understanding or spiritual comprehension of that which is within thine own realm or ken.

When these then are used or abused, in such manners as to be used only for self indulgencies, self-aggrandizement, the fruits of these must be contention and strife, inharmony and the like.

As has ever been in all experiences, like begets like. For, the purposes, the desires, are both spiritual and carnal, and as to the soul development of same is as to what are the fruits of such activities. "By their fruits ye shall know them," whether they be of those that make for tares in the experiences of the souls of men, or whether they be of wheat or some other grain that maketh for an increase in the activities of such individuals in their associations with their fellow man. For, in the material world may there only be used in spirit that which creates for the spiritual life. And as ye do unto your fellow man, so may the activity of the individual be in that line, as to whether it fulfils those purposes for which it came into being, with those talents that have been developed through the experiences of the entity in its application of truth, life and understanding to material things.

(Q) *How can Mrs. Garrett develop her ability to the highest degree?*

(A) By keeping self in accord in the inner self with that which is the highest that may manifest itself through the abilities and faculties of the soul body. Thus may it give to the seeker, thus may it give to those that would knock; for, as He has promised ever, if ye seek in the light of thine understanding, trusting in Him for the increase, so may this attitude being kept ever within self make for self being that channel through which only the constructive influences may come into the experience of the seeker.

(Q) *Do Mrs. Garrett's psychic powers depend on previous development? If so, describe the development which made this present manifested ability possible.*

(A) As has been indicated, depends upon much that has been soul development of the entity. And during those experiences when there were those in the lands now known as the Arabian and Persian, when there was the comprehension of the application of the truths in the spiritual relations of the souls of men, with the constructive influences in the activities of individuals, during those days and periods when those activities known as the Zoroastrian were active in the peoples of the land. The entity then was not only an instructor, a teacher, one that gave much to aid peoples at that period when the fires of life had burned low, but the entity made for the awakening within the hearts and minds of many those relationships that should exist between the creative influences in the spiritual realms with the activities among men. Hence a guide, a teacher, that aided much in those experiences, aids in manifesting to those that seek to see materializations of those forces that would make for presenting of lessons, of tenets, of the various theses of understanding in the experiences of individuals.

(Q) *Who are Mrs. Garrett's spiritual guides, and tell us something about them?*

(A) Let them rather speak for themselves through that channel that is capable rather of presenting them in their light to that which has been the development of the soul itself in its experiences in the earth in the realms of their activity. For, their names are rather in *her* experience, in *her* seeking, than to find through other channels; even though they may be coming from the records that are made by each in their activity. Speak for thyself.

(Q) *What counsel have you for Mrs. Garrett's spiritual development?*

(A) Present self in thine own inner conscience in such a way and manner that answers for the conscience within self of its own soul development. And as the soul remains true to that which is its ideal from within, it may never give that other than constructive in its speech with those that seek to know the mysteries of soul and self-development; that has made of itself a channel through which men may approach those mysteries of life, and their activities in the minds, the hearts and the souls of men.

(Q) *Is Mrs. Garrett contacting the highest possible sources for information in accordance with her development?*

(A) As the soul seeks, higher and higher may be those influences of the activities in the experience for the *development* of others in *their* approach to such realms. When the soul seeks for self, for self's own protection and for self's own activities, it reaches the highest that is for that soul's development. When the self is open to those that would question or would counsel with, dependent upon the desire, the purposes, the aims, as to from what source or channel; as it does for *any* soul that has opened itself for the activities of those influences that are in and about a material world. Yet for the self, for the soul's protection, for the abilities, it seeks, it contacts that which is sufficient unto the needs of the soul in its development.

(Q) *Is there any way in which Mrs. Garrett may be of special service to the work of Edgar Cayce?*

(A) As their channels of activity cross or run one into another, in the various phases of experience, there may be those aids that will be for the common good of all. Rather than that it may aid any individual work as of Edgar Cayce or any other source. Rather those who give themselves (as both may be found to be doing) for the common good of mankind, as they merge in their efforts in these directions, may there be the aids rather one for the other. For, as has been given, in the union there is strength; whether this be applied in those things pertaining to the least in the earth or the greater in the realm of the spiritual activity. Hence, as each in clear purpose of desire to be of aid to their fellow man, not for self—but that the glory of God may be manifested in the hearts and souls of men, *thus* may each aid the other. For, as He has given, whether in body, in mind or spirit, ye come seeking to make known the love of the Father in the earth to the sons of men, ye may aid one another.

(Q) *Would you explain why Edgar Cayce uses this method of hypnosis for going into trance?*

(A) That as has oft been given, from the physical development, or physical–mental development of the body, it has become necessary that there be the entire removal of the physical forces and physical attributes from the mental and spiritual and soul forces of the entity, to seek that through that built in the *soul*-body of the entity it may contact that which may be constructive in the experiences of those to whom such sources or such supplies of information may be brought.

(Q) *How did it arise? Was it accident, or some entity or group suggest this plan?*

(A) Soul development, rather. And the ability to, through those experiences in the earth in the varied activities, lay aside the consciousness that the soul and the spirit and the truth might find its way through to the seeker.

(Q) *Do you suggest that trance is a useful method for help?*

(A) Trance to the individual is as the necessary stimuli for each soul in its own development. There be those who may through their intuitive activity, that has subjugated the influences in the material, allow the mental soul to manifest. There be those who through looking into the past, or into the aura, or into all or any of those things that are as witnesses about every soul that walks through this vale. For, those that may lay aside the veil, in whatever form or manner, may make for the approach of aiding those in seeking to know that necessary in their development in the present experience.

(Q) *If Edgar Cayce has ever had controls, does he know who they are?*

(A) Anyone may speak who may seek, if the entity or the soul's activities will allow same; or if the desire of the individuals seeking so over commands as to make for a set channel.

(Q) *Is Edgar Cayce clairvoyant in the hypnotic state?*

(A) More so in the normal or physical state than in the hypnotic state; though *all* are one when in perfect accord with the universal forces from which the records of all activities may be taken.

(Q) *If Edgar Cayce goes into trance without any control, could he not in a waking state get the inspiration direct?*

(A) Not until there has been a more perfect cleansing of the carnal influences in the experiences of the soul, as has been indicated. With the regeneration that should come into the experience of the entity, this then may be the manner, the channel, the way through which much of constructive forces may be given.

(Q) *What entity is giving this information now?*

(A) Being directed, as has been indicated, from the records through Halaliel.

We are through.

5

●

Cayce on Telepathy

Text of Reading 792-2

This Psychic Reading given by Edgar Cayce at his home on Arctic Crescent, Virginia Beach, Va., this 6th day of May, 1937, in accordance with request made by the Research Group on the Work of the Ass'n for Research & Enlightenment, Inc., through Hugh Lynn Cayce.

PRESENT

Edgar Cayce; Gertrude Cayce, Conductor; Gladys Davis, Steno. Dorothy Jones, Pat Miller, Malcolm H. Allen, Hugh Lynn Cayce, Myrtle Demaio and Margaret Wilkins.

READING

Time of Reading 4:40 to 5:20 P.M.

GC: You will have before you the group of individuals who have been attempting elementary experiments in telepathy and card guessing on Thursday evenings in connection with the general work of the Ass'n for Research and Enlightenment, Inc. Members of this group are present here. We desire to make our experiments of practical value, if possible, to each member of the group in relation to the individual mental and spiritual development and also make whatever contribution our development permits to the general knowledge of the laws of telepathy and simple clairvoyance. You will advise us regarding the right or proper procedure to obtain the best possible results. Questions.

EC: Yes, we have the questions, we have the individuals, and those conditions that make same applicable in the experiences of those who have joined in the experiments thus far.

In the study of the phenomena of this nature, there should be first the questions and answers—or the analysis as to purpose—not only in the minds of those who would lend themselves in such an experience but in the minds of those who would preserve or present such experiments as a part of the research work of such an organization as the Association for Research and Enlightenment. As in this manner:

What is expected? What is the *source* of the information as may be had in such experiments, that goes beyond that called or termed the ordinary mind guessing? Or what is the basis of telepathic or clairvoyant communication? Or what are these in their elemental activity, or in all activity?

To be sure, the experience is a portion of the Mind; but Mind, as we have given, is both material *and* spiritual.

Now: From what order, or from what basis then, is such information sought by those who join in such experiments?

It is the basis of all relationship of the individual entity to the cosmic or the universal forces. Or, to make it simple—yet most complex: "Know—the Lord thy God is *One!*" *Know* the Lord thy God is *One!*"

Then the communications or the abilities for the activity of the Mind of an entity in such an experiment are *not* because of, or from, an association of entities.

It is not then to be presumed, supposed, or proposed, to be a calling upon, a depending upon, a seeking for, that which is without—or that outside of self; but rather the attuning of self to the divine within, which is (the divine) a universal or *the* universal consciousness.

This is proposed then as the basis for such investigation, and those who accredit or seek or desire other sources—Well, keep their records separate, and the more oft they will be found to be such as those that are patterns or examples in Holy Writ; namely, an excellent one Saul, the first king. Here we find an example of an individual seeking from the man of God, or the prophet, information to be given clairvoyantly, telepathically (if you choose to use such terms); and we find the incident used as an illustration that may be well kept to the forefront in the Minds of those who would prompt or check or record such experiments.

As to making practical application; it is what you do with the abilities that are developed by this attunement in coordinating, cooperating one with another in such experiments.

There are those in the group who have experimented that are gifted; gifted meaning then *innately* developed by the use of those faculties of the Mind to attune themselves to the Infinite.

Also there are those who have attuned themselves to a consciousness *not* wholly within themselves, but *prompted* by those who would become prompters—as in *any* attunement that is ever attempted in material consciousness, it is subject to same.

Then there is to be the proper consideration, or the proper evaluation of that which is gained by the experience of each that joins in with same.

This may be set as a criterion to any—yes, to all: When such an experiment, such a trial, draws or tires, or makes the mind faggy or dull or become as a drain upon the physical energies, know you are attuning wrong—and static has entered, from *some* source!

For the universal consciousness *is* constructive, not destructive in *any* manner—but ever constructive in its activity with the elements that make up an entity's experience in the physical consciousness.

Ready for questions.

(Q) Please suggest the type of experiments which may be conducted most successfully by this group.

(A) Well, you would have to take each as an individual—to say as to which may be the most successful! For there are grades, there are variations. These are in the group, as has been indicated, curiosity, wisdom, folly, *and* those things that make for real spiritual development. They each then require first—*first*—self-analysis! *what* prompts the individual to seek, engage, or desire to join in such experiments? As to how far, as to what—there is no end! Is there any end to infinity? For this is the attunement, then—to Infinity!

Each will find a variation according to the application and the abilities of each to become less and less controlled by personality, and the more and more able to shut away the material consciousness—or the mind portion that is of the material, propagated or implied by what is termed the five senses. The more and more each is impelled by that which is intuitive, or the relying upon the soul force within, the greater, the farther, the deeper, the broader, the more constructive may be the result.

More and more, then, turn to those experiments that are not only helpful but that give hope to others, that make for the activity of the fruits of the Spirit.

Make haste slowly.

Wait on the *Lord*; not making for a show, an activity of any kind that would be self–glorification, self–exaltation, but rather that which is help-ful, hopeful for others.

(Q) As each name is called, please give suggestions for that particular individual in carrying on his or her part of this group work: First, [1406].

(A) This entity's experience and experiments will only be altered or hindered by self, and it may go as far into the field as is desired—so long as it keeps God and Christ *as* the ideal. Whenever there is the entering of other entities, or consciousnesses, or personalities—be mindful of the ensample as is shown. Study that life, in association with such. Lose self more and more in the Christ Consciousness, if you would gain in those activities as may be thine, as may be seen by the soul development of this entity.

To each there is given the influence or spirit of direction.

To some there is given the interpretation of tongues, or the interpre-tation of words or signs or symbols. This is what is meant by interpret-ers of tongues in the Holy Writ.

To some is given healing; to some is given exhortation; to some is given ministration; to some is given one thing, some another.

Or, the *attunement* is the clarifier, or that which makes for clearer ac-cord with that phase of the phenomena called clairvoyance, telepathy, or any psychic force of an entity.

In this particular body, we will find *any* of these—but the *most* will be given in healing, by the laying on of hands.

(Q) [1431]:

(A) In exhortation; or attunements by discernment of activity—the application of individual self to such attunements.

Keep self towards not a *selfish* development, not a curious development, not for a famous development, but towards an *humbleness* of heart, an *humbleness* of purpose.

For if you would know the truth, you must humble yourself; and then—as the experiments in the ability of attunements come—we may find self given more and more in exhortation; not exaltation, but exhortation.

(Q) [303]:

(A) Here we find more and more that of a fearfulness, a hindrance by the holding to a physical consciousness. If there is the loss of self then to any extent, the physical consciousness, the deeper or better self may be given especially to bringing knowledge, understanding to others. For these are gained in self by giving out that you have. This is the secret of the whole process. You do not have until you give. You don't give to have, but you have because you give!

(Q) [562]:

(A) Hold fast to the self within.

These all present different problems within their inner self for development, for hindrances, and for possibilities. To be sure, all of these suggestions are given from the constructive angle, with the hopes that none will—as Saul—partake of same for self's own indulgence, or self's own glory.

But let the light, the *love divine*, be the guide; and we may find that those messages as for direction, as for help, may be thine.

(Q) [573]:

(A) Again the warning not to look back, nor look to the *emotions* that arise from the sensitiveness of the sensory forces of the body; but rather to that which arises from the spiritual concept of an ideal. Thus we will find that visions of helpful warnings, of helpful admonitions, of helpful conditions for experiences that arise in the lives of others, may be thy part.

(Q) [1226]:
(A) There is the tendency for worldly wisdom to confound the spiritual concept. Hence most of the common experiences become guesses, or the attempt to vision by mental–material visioning.

Turn loose of self, then may the entity indeed by a teacher, a minister, to those who are weak, to those who are self-wise.

But hold fast to Christ *in God;* and ye in Him! For as He has given, "As ye abide in me," so may there be brought to *your* remembrance that necessary for thy soul development, from the foundations of the earth. For if the Lord is One, and ye are one with Him, then it is as the current runs; or thy oneness with Him, as to the extent of thy ability to guide, direct, or to encourage those who are weak or lost in confusion of the times. Then with same, as in directing, will be healing.

(Q) [341]:
(A) Keep hold on Him ever as thou hast seen and heard. "Is not this Him of whom the prophets spoke?" Thus ye will find that not the worldly wise, not the material or the physical consciousness, but the awareness of divine love will enable thee to help, direct, and hold in check, those tendencies for material expression from disincarnate entities.

We are through—for the present.

Editor's Note: Dr. [1135] was a psychologist and received three readings on telepathy.

Text of Reading 1135-4 M 35 (Psychologist)

This psychic reading given by Edgar Cayce at the Kahn home, 44 West 77th St., Apt. 14-W, New York City, this 9th day of April, 1936, in accordance with request made by the self— Dr. [1135], Associate Member of the Ass'n for Research & Enlightenment, Inc.

PRESENT

Edgar Cayce; Gertrude Cayce, Conductor; Gladys Davis, Steno. Dr. [1135], Mrs. [1136] and Hugh Lynn Cayce.

READING
Time of Reading 4:10 to 4:35 P.M. Eastern Standard Time.

([1135], his intent and desire to conduct specific experiments with the
view of enlarging our understanding of thought transference (Mental
Telepathy). You will advise him regarding the best procedure to follow,
including basic principles and suggestions for properly conducting the
individual experiments.)

EC: Yes, we have the body and the enquiring mind; purposes, desires,
and those conditions that we find are relative to such activity in the
experience of others.

In considering conditions conducive to such an experience in the
activities of individuals, there are three phases or three elements that
go to make up the basic ideas or basic conditions that become relative
or co-related to such experience.

First, the Physical; then the Spiritual; and then the Processive Manners.

In the first process there are from the pathological standpoint or
view those elements in the first cause, or in the eugenics of that cause,
that produce in the plasm the vibratory rates that go to make for the
urge that produces itself through its relative activity to itself in its process—or the very nature physically or pathologically of the man, or
portion of the animal in its activity.

These are basic forces that make for the process of the activity of
relative thought, or primary interest, or a receptivity, or the ability to
become—as it were—subject to those very influences that go to produce
same.

Just as may be seen in certain necessary influences or forces that go
to make for conductors of energies used for transmissions of this or that
influence that may become active. Some are good conductors, some are
bad. Hence the physical force—these processes, these conditions are to
be considered in making the study of, or in producing the ideal setting
for such an activity.

Then the spiritual, or the intent, the purpose, the influence that possesses such a house, such a body; not merely from the physical the

tangible intelligencia of the activity, but the purpose and intent and desire of that manifesting through same; whether it, that activity, of the spirit, is in that process of its own ego or that merely as the channel for those expressions that may be as an activity in such a process.

If these are of the nature that they are for, or have as their keynotes, the exploitation or self-indulgence or self-aggrandizement of the man's activity, then they must eventually become as those influences that would destroy the very influence that would be activative through such a channel.

Then the process, as indicated, in knowing, in realizing or classifying those that are from their very natures those subjects for such an activity. And those influences as indicated should be the basis for such attempts for the creative force or activity of that which is indeed the psychic force. For here, as indicated by the very term itself, the spirit or soul of the entity or individual (not the personality but the individuality of those that are in accord or may be attuned) is active. Not all elements may be attuned to a vibratory influence sufficient for sending or receiving. Some may send while others may receive. There may be those that are able to do both.

And such activities make for, then, a unison that becomes coordinant in its every relationship.

First, then, what are the necessary forces, the necessary elements? Or what would be the vibratory rate of individuals that may be said to be chosen as susceptible to attunement? Those that would be called emotional, or those staid? Those that would be easily moved by the influences about them, or those that remain malleable to influences of every nature?

What would be the pulse rate, the heart beat, the vibratory forces of the body-influence itself?

There must be, from that indicated, an ideal relationship in such, from the purely mechanical or the purely material viewpoint.

Those in which the ratio of those cycles about each of the red blood corpuscles is one to three. Those whose body-vibratory forces are eighty-seven and seven-tenths (87 and 7/10). Those having a pulsation that would range from the normalcy of a seventy-two to seventy-eight and six tenths (72 to 78 and 6/10).

These are the physical activities that become necessary for a consideration that may be had in same.

All such would be found to respond to normal reflexes; that their activity in making for the vibrations through the influences of the lyden upon the pineal becomes a normal reaction; that they are negative to influences that arise from any infectious or insidious force that may have been a portion of the impregnation from the very firm [?] [vermiform?] or first activity of the effluvium in its creative influence.

These would be, then, the physical processes that would be for the beginning—or the basic force. Then those that would be of the nature that their thought, their intent, is not by self acclamation but by activity less thoughtful of self than of their duties, obligations, dependencies, influences—[Hugh Lynn Cayce got up, starting to leave the room, and the reading stopped.]

We are through for the present.

Text of Reading 1135-5 M 35 (Psychologist)

This psychic reading given by Edgar Cayce at his home on Arctic Crescent, Virginia Beach, Va., this 6th day of May, 1936, in accordance with request made by the self—Dr. [1135], Associate Member of the Ass'n for Research & Enlightenment, Inc.

PRESENT

Edgar Cayce; Gertrude Cayce, Conductor; Gladys Davis, Steno. Hugh Lynn Cayce.

READING

Time of Reading 4:30 to 4:40 P.M. Eastern Standard Time. New York City.

(Continue information given through this channel for [1135] on Mental Telepathy on April 9, 1936, under the following suggestion: Consider the intent and desire of [1135] to conduct specific experiments with the view of enlarging our understanding of thought transference (Mental Telepathy). Advise regarding the best procedure to follow, including basic principles and suggestions for properly conducting the individual experiments.)

EC: Yes.

Then, as the physical or pathological and mental conditions have been given, in what manner would or should be the procedure in understanding or applying such laws to be studied or to be contacted?

That the phenomenon is of the high mental forces, or what may be termed the superconscious forces; and not using the ordinary means but that such conditions found to be existent in specific individuals are *attuned* to the various forms or manners of giving manifestations of same. Then these may not be tested for their efficiency or for their value in the practical experience in your test tubes or other ordinary means or measures, but must be upon the basis or direction in which these take their bent or trend.

For an illustration:

You find an artiste that is musical; with the ear and sense forces given for the application in the use of some specific instrument. Do you give one that's playing a horn piano lessons? or piano lessons to one that plays the violin?

Not that these are not kindred. Not that these are not in accord. But the expression, the ability to move those forces that manifest themselves, comes through their *particular* phase of expression and manner.

Thus in seeking these, find first, take first, those of the pathological; then their correlations with the sincerity or the honesty of the individual and their correlated effects or activity in the spiritual force. Then follow these in their varied channels. And there may be found, there may be discovered in many much that is not only worthy of acceptation but that will make for the abilities of many—that have been attempted to be made into this or that in the developing of their activities through their expression in a given experience—to find *themselves* and thus give expression to that which is in the *inner* sense the telepathic communication of their real selves to that in another realm or material realm.

Ready for questions.

(Q) *Please explain what is meant by the ratio of those cycles about each of the red blood corpuscles is one to three? How determined?*

(A) By taking the blood itself of individuals and making that count as to what is the protoplasmic cellular force given off by such individuals.

(Q) *The one to three refers to what relationship?*

(A) Positive and negative cycle forces about each atomic structure in the blood cell itself.

(Q) *What is referred to by the body-vibratory forces 87 and 7/10? How may this be determined?*

(A) The number of the pulsations or the opening and shutting forces of the coordinating of the blood supply between lung, heart and liver.

(Q) *How may that be determined?*

(A) Count it, as it acts through the system!

(Q) *In order to gain a better understanding of this subject [1135] has proposed in a letter from him under date of April 26th—*

(A) (Interrupting) Then let him do something about it! We are *through*!

[Following portion of question was not asked due to interruption: "a copy of which I hold in my hand, that an experiment be undertaken through this channel and under the observation of professors from Columbia University. a. Observation of any experiment suggested through this channel. (or) b. Undertake an experiment devised by [1135]."]

[Other questions submitted which did not get asked:

"As indicated [1135] proposes not to connect the name of Cayce or the Association with the results if we so desire at this time. He feels that this step will lead to considerable light on this subject and the possibility of him being able to devote more time to a direct study of this work, in connection with Duke University activities.

"Regarding telepathy:

"1. In attempting to send a mental impression is it best that the sender hold a picture of the word or impression to be transferred or hold the name of the image or impression in mind? What would be the easiest symbols to send? Do you recommend any special type of symbol or impression for experimental purposes? 2. What part does the time element play in transference of thought? What part do physical surroundings, position of the body, and condition of the physical body play in transference of thought? 3. Explain what takes place when a thought passes from one mind to another."]

Text of Reading 1135-6 M 36 (Psychologist)

This psychic reading given by Edgar Cayce at the home of David E. Kahn, 20 Woods Lane, Scarsdale, N.Y., this 11th day of November, 1936, in accordance with request made by Dr. [1135], Associate Member, and Hugh Lynn Cayce, Manager, of the Ass'n for Research & Enlightenment, Inc., Virginia Beach, Va.

PRESENT

Edgar Cayce; Gertrude Cayce, Conductor; Gladys Davis, Steno. Dr. [1135] and his son [1177].

READING

Time of Reading 3:40 to 4:00 P.M. Eastern Standard Time.

GC: We seek at this time to prepare for a series of readings to be used as a basis for arousing sufficient interest for some University, perhaps Duke or Columbia, to appoint [1135] present in this room, as a special investigator to undertake an extended observation and collection of material already furnished through this channel. We feel that a thorough study of the psychic phenomena as manifested through this channel will contribute much to a scientific knowledge of psychic laws. [1135] presents himself at this time seeking, in cooperation with the Management of the Association and Edgar Cayce, present here, suggestions and advice on this proposal. You will answer questions.

EC: In considering such a series of tests and the like, that which has been given as to the purpose or the intent should be considered first.

As we find, if there is an extensive study made as the information is given for individuals under the varied circumstances who present themselves for such help or aid as may be had through these channels, this would supply any question that may arise in the minds of those who seek in or from the spiritual and mental angle for the determining of the value of such information in the experience of individuals.

There may be specific tests in Mind Reading, Telepathy, Thought Transference, Moving of Objects even; yet these when presented out of their realm of activity dealing with the individual for a helpful experience in the seeking, become channels that are of an entirely different nature—and partake, as we have given, either of subconscious impressions or the activities of consciousnesses in the realm of the inter-between that would become as detrimental to the value of such information in the experience of consecrated seeking individuals for their aid and help to an understanding of their relationships to Creative Forces in this particular experience.

Hence the manner as we would find that there should be the study: Take the information, the data, or the regular routine of seekers. Find their relationships, their mental attitudes, their desires, their hopes. And then watch the effect of the varied status of condition or development, first of the individual and then the effects that are produced in the lives of such individuals. Not only from the purely physical angle but the moral, the mental and the spiritual activities and relations of same in the individual's experience.

And if these, or a series, or a continuation of the studies of such would be undertaken by one such as we find as has been indicated—as [1135]—we would find there may be almost every form of psychic phenomena and psychic experience.

For as we have given, there are almost as many types of psychic phenomena or psychic experience as there are individuals.

For *psychic* is of the soul, if in its true constructive sense. And as the soul is an individual, intricate portion of the whole, then the experience of each soul in its reaction with, upon or from experiences in that field of activity, presents a study within itself.

This then as we find should be rather that to any group or any university:

There be presented what has been the experience of individuals taken in every way and manner that have been recorded by the Association and those interested in same. If these do not present sufficient truth, sufficient confidence of there being not only the unusual but that which the individuals applying—not merely knowing of but applying in their experience day by day—will make them as individuals better citizens, better neighbors, better parents, better friends, then forget it!

For unless such experiences create such in the lives of individuals that interest or apply themselves in the study of such, then it is indeed of little thought; nor has it any place in man's experience, and is not worthy of a name or consideration of *any* sort—or of any soul.

Then, these are the manners as we would give for the consideration:

If experiments are sought, these then must be weighed in the light of that given.

Many an individual, many a personage has given his all for the demonstrating of a truth. As it has been indicated from the first through *this* channel, there should ever be that ideal, "What does such information as may come through such a channel produce in the experience of individuals, as to not their thoughts, not their relations other than does such make them better parents, better children, better husbands, better wives, better neighbors, better friends, better citizens?" And if and when it does *not, leave it alone*!

Ready for questions.

(Q) [1135] presents the following plan. Advise us if this may be undertaken through this channel. The plan: Please describe contents of package on filing case in Room 215, Schermerhorn Extension, Columbia University, N.Y.

(A) This may be done; and if [1135] and those of the Association and their ideals and officers consider it worth it to be done, it will be done!

But *remember*—what has been given!

We are through.

Editor's Note: In a reading for Mr. [2533], who led a small group of people who were seeking to develop their telepathic abilities, Cayce gave the following guidance.

Reading 2533–7

(Q) Give these entities the principle and technique of conscious telepathy.

(A) The consciousness of His abiding presence. For, He is all power, all thought, the answer to every question. For, as these attune more and more to the awareness of His presence, the desire to know of those influences that may be revealed causes the awareness to become materially practical.

First, begin between selves. Set a definite time, and each at that moment put down what the other is doing. Do this for twenty days. And ye will find ye have the key to telepathy.

Editor's Note: Mr. [341] asked how best to develop his telepathic ability.

Reading 341-16

(Q) How can this body best develop these mental telepathic conditions?

(A) By knowing first laws as pertains to same, especially as in relation to individual self, and this will be gained better by understanding the urges from each earthly appearance, correlated with urges in the present day experiences, see? for as the entity finds, telepathic forces as manifest at present are relative to those with whom entity has contacted in the sphere of some mental development in the material world. Find those all first.

Editor's Note: Ms. [1500] asked if she had any clairvoyant ability.

Reading 1500-4

(Q) Have I any clairvoyant powers which could be developed?

(A) *Every* entity has clairvoyant, mystic, psychic powers. This entity, owing to its indicated developments, has clairvoyant *and* psychic powers. The intuitional, which is both clairvoyant *and* psychic, is the higher development; and this may be applied in the teaching—which has been indicated as an experience through which greater expression of self may be given than in most fields. If this is used in the application of metaphysical interpretations, it will be the better for self, and the entity itself may make same more practical in the experience of those she attempt to teach or direct.

But ever know the source of thy information, that it is in the metaphysical or intuitional experience of the souls that may attune to the spiritual or creative force from within—and there *is* an advocate with the Father. The promise is in that He gave, "Lo, I am with you—always!"

(Q) What steps should I take to accomplish this?

(A) First, it must be lived, desired, practiced within self, in its dealings with its fellow man. Do not teach that which is only theory. *Live* in thy own experience that thou would teach thy neighbor, thy brother.

(Q) Is my future work to be accomplished with Metaphysics?

(A) This depends upon the choice of self. As just indicated, this may be made a more expressive channel through which activities may be made to bring the greater peace and harmony within the experience of self.

(Q) What special line?

(A) This again must be a choice. It should be along greater spiritual lines, if there would be the assurance ever within self. That it may take on at times great healing abilities is not to be sought ether than as He gives the expression—that which is in the experience of all; to some it is given to be exhorters, to others teachers, to others healers by laying on of hands, others healers by prayer, to one the interpreting of tongues, to another the speech by tongues—but all of the same Spirit, the consciousness of the Christ abiding within self. Not only by acclaim but by practical application of the Christ-Spirit in thy daily walks, thy daily talks; and thy dealings with thy fellow man.

Let him that approacheth then the throne of service do so rather in that attitude that may be expressed in this—in thine *own* words:

Here am I, O God! Use Thou me in the manner, in the channels, in the ways that I may the better—through the love Thou hast shown me in the gift of the promises in the Christ—glorify Thee before my fellow man!

Editor's Note: Mr. [440] learned from Cayce that certain stones could "step up" the body's ability for telepathy.

Reading 440-18

(Q) You will examine the [lapis] stones which I hold, telling which is the most powerful for the various uses it may be used for. You will explain these various uses and recommend those that would be most helpful.

(A) In giving that which may be helpful it is necessary, for this mind or body seeking same, that there be rather the analysis of the composition of the stones as related to their vibrations—as relate then to a human body, see?

Either of these shows a variation of their composition; as to the elements of those influences that make for vibrations in the ether as related to that which may be effective in drawing to or disseminating from—through, of course, the vibrations being those that are of the positive and negative natures in the very stone itself—making for, then, the analysis; knowing same by what is called the constituents of it, through the mineralogy, the activity through those channels themselves. We would then find that the one that is the nearer in accord to the vibrations of the body that may use same would be the more effective with *that* particular body. Yet the very *nature* of the thing makes it effective with any—*any*—human body, you see; but the more effective with one that is more in accord, or whose positive and negative vibrations are according with the stone itself, see? for it throws off as well as draws in, you see, through the positive–negative vibration. This assists, then, in the unison as a relationship. This is as a comparison—don't confuse it and say that it is electricity; it is electrical, of course, in its vibration, but as the stone in its vibration, is then in sympathy with a body that is also sympathetic—or may be said to be *sensitive*—it assists in "stepping up" the sensitiveness of the body as would the electrical vibration in an alternating force step up by the addition of influences or forces of electrical vibration being thrown off from other channels in making it more powerful. See? Towards what? Towards the effectiveness in its sensitiveness (that is, the body) as to what it maybe seeking. Hence, as given of old, use such for the abilities to become more of all those influences called in the present psychic, clairaudient or any of those vibrations that build up or "step up" a body. Also effective, of course, in bringing to the body the abilities to become more effective in giving out of itself for activity in any of these various directions.

(Q) *Which of the three stones, then, is better suited to my vibrations?*

(A) The one in the center. [8/2/35 See EC's letter under 813-1 saying he was with (440) in Arizona when (440) found a lapis stone in a mine several hundred feet under the ground.]

(Q) *This one?*

(A) This one.

(Q) *Why were these stones mentioned to me in the beginning?*

(A) They are as those things of old, which if followed (and the body was seeking at the time for those things) may be used as stepping-stones for the understanding of vibrations as related to the mineral forces and as to man.

(Q) *Are these as fine specimens of "lapis lingua" that can be obtained?*

(A) As fine as may be obtained in the present for the demonstrating of, or for the use in relation to, these very things as given.

Editor's Note: From Edgar Cayce's perspective, dreams were often a source of telepathic communication, as in these next readings.

Text of Reading 900-314 M 32
(Stockbroker, Jewish)

This Psychic Reading given by Edgar Cayce at his office, 115 West 35th Street, Virginia Beach, Va., this 18th day of April, 1927, in accordance with request made by self—Mr. [900].

P R E S E N T

Edgar Cayce; Mrs. Cayce, Conductor; Gladys Davis, Steno. Hugh Lynn Cayce.

R E A D I N G

Time of Reading 11:40 A.M. Eastern Standard Time. New York City.

GC: You will have before you the body and the enquiring mind of [900], of . . . St., N.Y. City, and the dreams this body had on the dates which I will give you. You will give the interpretation and lesson to be gained from each of these, as I read them to you, and you will answer the questions which I will ask you regarding same.

EC: Yes, we have the body, the enquiring mind, [900]. This we have had here before. We find again those presentations to the various phases of the consciousness of the entity presented in emblematical manners for the instruction of the body mind of the entity. Ready for dream.

(Q) Morning of April 15, 1927. Saw Hugh Lynn Cayce home from college. "Aren't you going back to college?" I asked him. "No," he replied, reclining on a sofa. "Hugh Lynn is going to take my old position," (It seemed in Detroit or another city) interrupted Mrs. Cayce. She looked daggers at me and I felt she blamed me for many things and was holding in her mind much that she would like to tell me, not particularly complimentary either. She was very angry with me for something and I wondered why and wished I might change that.

(A) In this we find again that illustration of telepathic conditions, as are termed, from mind to mind, and with the entity's consciousness subjugated, with the thought, intent and purport of same directed to-ward those conditions in which the body conscious is so wrapped up, the entity gains those impressions of the condition through which the mental mind of the body seen is passing. Not only gaining that concept of the mind that is in that turmoil as seen but, as well, those conditions that will be presented to other minds as seen as regarding position, see? Hence we have these conditions as *things*, as has been given that thoughts are deeds, or things, and may become miracles or crimes—as seen in the vision that one looks as if it would like to use daggers—for in that is as purely mental. Not that there is any condition of misunder-standing between the two. Rather that turmoil through which the mind of one seen is passing, on account of conditions as were understood, or as were viewed in the mind of the body as seen, see? The lesson, then, is rather to the entity that of another phase of consciousness as is pre-sented to the entity, and may be studied or used as an illustration of what is meant as thought or telepathic transference of one mind to another, and is to be studied only in that light, see?

(Q) *Is there any hard feeling in the relationship between these two, [900] and Mrs. Cayce?*

(A) No hard relationship, other than that of not full comprehending the intent and purport of each as they contact the efforts of the work; yet, as is seen from that presented, both may gain and be beneficial to each in their respective sphere of association with same, or—as is seen again—that each taking an inactive or indirect part in same may bring destructive forces to each and to themselves, see? These are not, then, as contradictory, but these may be builded as something that is above the ordinary in their relationships to each, see? for, as is seen, there is easily the bond of sympathy that will assist each, were they to develop same—to illustrate, very easily, telepathic communication, see?

Text of Reading 900-139 M 30 (Stockbroker, Jewish)

This psychic reading given by Edgar Cayce at his office, 35th Street, Virginia Beach, Va., this 10th day of October, 1925, in accordance with request made by self—Mr. [900].

PRESENT

Edgar Cayce; Mr. Cayce, Conductor; Gladys Davis, Steno.

READING

Time of Reading 3:15 P.M. Eastern Standard Time. New York City.

GC: You will have before you the body and the enquiring mind of [900], of . . . , New York City, and the dreams this body had on the dates which I will give you. You will give the interpretation and lesson to be gained from each of these, as I read same to you, and will answer the questions which I will ask you regarding same.

EC: Yes, we have the enquiring mind of [900], with dreams as have and do come to the body from time to time. Ready for dream.

(Q) *Monday Morning, Sept. 21, at home in Deal. It seemed I was looking for a boarding house and found a room with a Mrs. Garagan. I went down town to tend to some political work and seemed to be doing some bartering or trading. I took a lump of gold that I thought worth $500 for the money, or instead of money itself. I entered a class room and a man, who it seemed was an old timer at politics, told me that I shouldn't have taken that lump of gold. Foolish to do so. After the election I went home to my boarding house, which I found closed. I looked around and saw a sign on the window "Mrs. Garagan moved across the street." I went across the street and found her. "Well," I said to her, putting down some papers I had and sitting down, "the election is over." Garagan, her son, was a politician, and I wanted to make the mother, Mrs. Garagan, feel good, so I told a lie, saying to her as she stood ironing: "You know, I told so and so that Garagan said that Walker—no I mean Waterman would be elected." She smiled and I indicated the gold lump I had. She nodded and as she put up her ironing board indicated the money might have been better. I stood up, gathered my papers and felt tired and bored in the drab boarding house. "What will I do now," I queried—the field seemed so limited and I was so tired. It seemed to darken and grow dreary.*

(A) Now, we find in the presentation in this dream, there are many different and various phases and stages of the development of the entity presented to the body, [900], in an emblematical manner that shows the development of same.

In the vision, the boarding house, is seen that of the telepathic presentation of the place, the surroundings, the conditions, under which the entity labors, and as the name Garagan indicates, carries, that rule under which a portion of the physical rule of place indicated by temperament, by mental ability, by physical force, as is also seen in the political work; yet the school again presenting the lesson or training to which the mind, the physical forces or body, may attain from the careful consideration, understanding and study of same. As again telepathic through the body–mind, with cosmic forces presented, in the names Walker, Waterman, as presented to the body. Hence we have many various portions of the mental forces of physical nature to be studied in this.

The lessons then, rather that of the study that the entity shall make of conditions physical, conditions cosmic, conditions spiritual, through which the entity labors, and as is seen with the gaining of information from other sources than the physical, brings the entity to that imperfect co–relation, unless co–related in its proper sphere with those who do not follow out all the phases of the various developments in the study of the phenomena as is presented to the body, as is seen in the return and inability to locate, until signs are read, see?

6

●

Cayce on the Psychic Atlanteans

Editor's Note: Edgar Cayce gave a series of readings on ancient Atlantis. In one of these readings he described how the Atlanteans were initially quite psychic, to the point that we could not understand them and their lives if we did not grasp just how psychic they were. Here is that reading. I believe it adds to our study of the psychic sense, especially since Cayce predicted that humanity would regain these powerful abilities in the near future.

Text of Reading 364-10

This psychic reading given by Edgar Cayce at his home in Pinewood on Lake Drive, Virginia Beach, Va., this 28th day of April, 1932, in accordance with request made by those present.

PRESENT

Edgar Cayce; Gertrude Cayce, Conductor; Gladys Davis, Steno. Mildred Davis, H.L. & L.B. Cayce.

READING

Time of Reading 3:00 P.M.

GC: You will have before you the information given through this channel on the lost continent of Atlantis. You will please continue with this information, and answer the questions which I will ask regarding same.

EC: Yes. In understanding, then, in the present terminology, occult science, or psychic science—as seen, this was the natural or nature's activity in that experience, and not termed a science—any more than would be the desire for food by a new born babe. Rather the natural consequence. This explanation may of necessity take on some forms that may possibly be confusing at times, but illustrations may be made through the various types of occult science, or psychic manifestations, that may clarify for the student something of the various types of psychic manifestations in the present, as well as that that was natural in this period.

There is, as has been oft given, quite a difference—and much differentiation should be made—in mysticism and psychic, or occult science as termed today.

From that which has been given, it is seen that individuals in the beginning were more of thought forms than individual entities with personalities as seen in the present, and their projections into the realms of fields of thought that pertain to a developing or evolving world of matter, with the varied presentations about same, of the expressions or attributes in the various things about the entity or individual, or body, through which such science—as termed now, or such phenomena as would be termed—became manifest. Hence we find occult or psychic science, as would be called at the present, was rather the natural state of man in the beginning. Very much as (in illustration) when a baby, or babe, is born into the world and its appetite is first satisfied, and it lies sleeping. Of what is its dreams? That it expects to be, or that it has been? Of what are thoughts? That which is to be, or that which has been, or that which is? Now remember we are speaking—these were thought forms, and we are finding again the illustrations of same!

When the mental body (Now revert back to what you are calling science)—when the mental body, or mind, has had training, or has gone through a course of operations in certain directions, such individuals are called so-and-so minded; as one of an inventive turn, and trained;

one of a statistician turn, and trained; one of a theologian turn, and trained; one of philosophical turn, and trained. Of what does the mind build? We have turned, then, to that that has become very material, for the mind constantly trained makes for itself *mental* pictures, or makes for that as is reasoned with from its own present dimensional viewpoints—but the babe, from whence its reasoning? from whence its dream? From that that has been taken in, or that that has been its experience from whence it came? Oft has it been said, and rightly, with a babe's smile 'Dreaming of angels', and close in touch with them—but what has *produced* that dream? The contact with that upon which *it* has fed! Don't forget our premise now from which we are reasoning! and we will find that we will have the premise from which those individuals, or the entities, reasoned within the beginning in this land. (We are speaking of Atlanteans, when they became as thought forces.) From whence did *they* reason? From the Creative Forces from which they had received their impetus, but acted upon by the thought *forms* as were in *material* forms about them, and given that power (will) to be one *with* that from what it sprang or was given its impetus, or force, yet with the ability to *use* that in the way that seemed, or seemeth, good or well, or pleasing, unto itself. Hence we find in this particular moulding or mouldive stage, that in which there was the greater development of, and use of, that as is termed or called psychic and occult forces, or science—in the present terminology, or age.

Illustrating, then, that as to how this was used by those entities, those beings, in the formative stage of their experience or sojourn among that as had been created in all of its splendor to supply every want or desire that might be called forth by that being, with all of its attributes physical, mental *and spiritual* at hand; for, as has been given, even unto the four hundred thousandth generation from the first creation was it prepared for man's indwelling. As we today (turn to today), we find there the developments of those resources. How long have they remained? Since the beginning! How long has man been able to use them for his undoing, or his pleasure, or for his regeneration? Since the knowledge of some source has awakened within its psychic force, or source, of the apparatus, or the form that it takes, either in a physical or mental (for remember, Mind is the Builder—and it moves along those channels through which, and by which, it may bring into existence in whatever dimension or sphere from which it is reasoning, or reasoning toward—see)—and as these may be illustrated in the present:

When there is a manifestation of a psychic force, or an occult action, or phenomena, or activity in, upon, of or for, an individual, there is then the rolling back, as it were, or a portion of the physical consciousness—or that mental trained individual consciousness—has been rolled aside, or rolled back, and there is then a visioning—To what? That as from the beginning, a projection *of* that form that assumed its position or condition in the earth as from the beginning, and with those so endowed with that as may be called an insight into psychic sources there may be visioned about a body its astral (if chosen to be termed), rather its *thought* body, as is projected *from* same in such a state; especially so when there is the induction, or the inducing of, an unconsciousness of the normal brain, or normal mental body. Submerged—into what? Into the unconscious, or subconscious. Sub, in *this* instance, meaning *below*—not above normal; below—*subjected* to the higher consciousness, or to the higher thought, that has been builded—just as sure as has a physical body been builded, from what? That as has been given from its first nucleus as passed through in its experience. Then there may be visioned by such a body, as may be called with the second sight, or with a vision, that accompanying thought body of such an one, manifesting in much the way and manner as individuals in the Atlantean period of psychic and occult development brought about in their experience. Through such projections there came about that first necessity of the division of the body, to conform to those necessities of that as seen in its own mental vision as builded (*mental* now—Don't confuse these terms, or else you will become *very* confused in what is being given!).

The mental vision by its action upon what body is being builded? On the mental body of the individual in a material world, out of Spirit, out of the ability to have all the attributes of the spiritual or unseen forces—but *materialized* forces, as is necessary from the mental body in a material world *mentally* trained to, or in, certain directions, or given directions, or following the natural bent of its threefold or three-ply body, as is seen in every individual or every entity. As these projected themselves, then we find these *developments* were in this portion of the development in the Atlantean period. How were these used? In much as were from the beginning. Remember there was ever the instruction to those peoples that were to hold to that that would bring for the spiritual forces, rather than the abuses of the abilities—as those with familiar spirits, as those that spoke to or partook of the divinations of those that had passed from the earth's plane, or those that partook of the animal magnetism—that came from the universal consciousness of animal matter as passed into its experience, in its interchange through those periods of integration and disintegration—and the spirit forces possessing those that would lay themselves open to such conditions, for these are as real as physical bodies if the attunements of the entity are such that it may vision them! and they are about you always, sure! These, then, are entities—sure; whether animal or those endowed with the soul—until they pass through those changes—as there ever has been, see? Also there are those that ever make for those channels in the psychic and occult (we are speaking of, through which man—as it reached that stage, or that position that it became farther and farther from its natural sources, through the same *character* of channel may it communicate with that from which it is a portion of, or the Creative Forces), and hence the terminology arose as "Good Spirits" and "Bad Spirits"; for there are those that partake of the earth, or of the carnal forces, rather than of those forces that are of the spiritual or *creative*. Those that are destruction are of the earth. Those that are constructive, then, are the good—or the divine and the devilish, bringing for those developments in their various phases. Hence the greater development of that called occult, or psychic forces, during the Atlantean period—and the use of same, and the abuse of same—was during its first thousand years, as we would call light years; not the light of the star, but the sun goes down and the sun goes down—years. That brought about those cycles, or those changes. Hence we have that which has been given through many of the sources of information, or the channels for individuals—and in those, these, the entity—as a voice upon waters, or as the wind that moved among the reeds and harkened, or again as when the morning stars sang together and the sons of God beheld the coming of man into his own, through the various realms as were brought by the magnifying of, or the deteriorating of, the use of those forces and powers as manifested them-

selves in a *material* area, or those that partook of carnal to the gratification of that that brought about its continual *hardening* and less ability to
harken back through that from *which* it came, and partaking more and
more *of* that upon which it became an eater of; or, as is seen even in the
material forces in the present: We find those that partake of certain
elements, unless these become very well balanced *with* all *sources*—Of
what? That of which there were the first causes, or nature, or natural, or
God's sources or forces are. Hence *elements*—not rudiments; elements—
as are termed in the terminology of the student of the anatomical, physiological, psychological forces within a body—*germs*! Sure they are germs!
for each are as atoms of power—From what? That source from which it
has drawn its essence upon what it feeds. Is one feeding, then, its soul?
or is one feeding its body? or is one feeding that interbetween (its mental body) to its own undoing, or to those foolishnesses of the simple
things of life? Being able, then, to partake *of* the physical but not a part
of same—but more and more feeding upon those sources from which it
emanates itself, or of the *spiritual* life, so that the physical body, the
mental body, are attuned *to* its soul forces, or its soul source, its Creator,
its Maker, in such a way and manner, as it develops.

What, then, *is* psychic force? What *is* occult science? A developing of
the abilities within each individual that has not lost its sonship, or its
relation to its Creator, to live upon—or demonstrate more and more
through phenomena of whatever nature from which it takes its source,
for that individual activity of that entity itself through the stages of
development through which it has passed, and giving of its life source
that there may be brought *into* being that which gives more knowledge
of the source *from* which the entity *essence* (Isn't a good word, but signi-
fies that intended to be expressed; not elements, not rudiments, but
essence of the entity itself, *its* spirit and soul—its spirit being its portion of
the Creator, its soul that of its entity itself, making itself individual, separate entity, that may be one *with* the Creative Force from which it
comes—or which it is! of which it is made up, in its atomic forces, or in
its very essence itself!) emanates; and the more this may be manifest,
the greater becomes the occult force.

To what uses, then, did these people in this particular period give
their efforts, and in what directions were they active? As many almost

as there were individuals! for, as we find from the records as are made, to some there was given the power to become the sons of God; others were workers in brass, in iron, in silver, in gold; others were made in music, and the instruments of music. These, then, we find in the world today (Today, now—we are reasoning from today). Those that are especially gifted in art—in its various forms; and a real artist (as the world looks at it) isn't very much fit for anything else! yet it is—What? An expression of its concept *of* that from *which* it, that entity, sprang—through the various stages of its evolution (if you choose to call it such) in a material world, or that which it fed its soul or its mental being for its development through its varied experiences *in* a material world. These, then, are but manifestations (occult forces) in individuals who are called geniuses, or gifted in certain directions.

These, then, are the manners in which the *entities*, those *beings*, those *souls*, in the beginning partook of, or developed. Some brought about monstrosities, as those of its (that entity's) association by its projection with its association with beasts of various characters. Hence those of the Styx, satyr, and the like; those of the sea, or mermaid; those of the unicorn, and those of the various forms—these projections of what? The abilities in the *psychic* forces (psychic meaning, then, of the mental *and* the soul—doesn't necessarily mean the body, until it's enabled to be brought *into* being in whatever form it may make its manifestation—which may never be in a material world, or take form in a three-dimensional plane as the earth is; it may remain in a fourth-dimensional—which is an idea! Best definition that ever may be given of fourth-dimension is an idea! Where will it project? Anywhere! Where does it arise from? Who knows! Where will it end? Who can tell! It is all inclusive! It has both length, breadth, height and depth—is without beginning and is without ending! Dependent upon that which it may feed for its sustenance, or it may pass into that much as a thought or an idea. Now this isn't ideal that's said! It's idea! see?)

In the use of these, then, in this material plane—of these forces—brought about those that made for all *manners* of the various forms that are used in the material world today, *many* of them to a much higher development. As those that sought forms of minerals—and being able to be that the mineral was, hence much more capable—in the psychic or

occult force, or power—to classify, or make same in its own classifica-
tions. Who classified them? They were from the beginning! They are
themselves! They were those necessities as were *in* the beginning from
an *all wise* Creator! for remember these came, as did that as was to be the
keeper of same! The husbandman of the vineyard! Each entity, each
individual—today, has its own vineyard to keep, to dress—For who? Its
Maker, from whence it came! What is to be the report in thine own life
with those abilities, those forces, as may be manifest in self—through its
calling upon, through what? How does prayer reach the throne of mercy
or grace, or that from which it emanates? From itself! Through that of
crucifying, nullifying, the carnal mind and opening the mental in such a
manner that the Spirit of truth may flow in its psychic sense, or occult
force, into the very being, that you may be one with that from which
you came! Be thou faithful unto that committed into thy keeping! Life
itself is precious! For why? It is of the Maker itself! That *is* the beginning!
The psychic forces, the attunements, the developments, going *to* that! As
did many in that experience. And Enoch walked with God, and he was
not for God took him. As was many of those in those first years, in this
land, this experience.

These in the present, then, do not justly call it science; rather being
close to nature. Listen at the birds. Watch the blush of the rose. Listen at
the life rising in the tree. These serve their Maker—Through what? That
psychic force, that *is* Life itself, in their respective sphere—that were put
for the service of man. Learn thine lesson, O Man, from that about thee!

We are through for the present.

**Editor's Note: For more on Cayce's view of Atlantis, see *Edgar Cayce on
Atlantis* and *Edgar Cayce's Atlantis*, both available through A.R.E. Press.**

7

●

Cayce's Perspective on Spirit Communication

Editor's Note: From Cayce's perspective, communicating with people who were not incarnate (spirits) was simply another aspect of the psychic sense. However, he was not a supporter of Ouija boards and séances, preferring communications of a more healthy nature and ones that did not lead to confusion about and distraction from a soul's incarnate purposes and relationships. Yet, as the following discourses will show, he taught that these spirit communications have a place in the full spectrum of life and the psychic sense.

Text of Reading 5756-4

This Psychic Reading given by Edgar Cayce at his office, 115 West 35th Street, Virginia Beach, Virginia, this 17th day of March, 1927, in accordance with request made by Edgar Cayce himself and [900].

PRESENT

Edgar Cayce; Gertrude Cayce, Conductor; Gladys Davis, Steno.

READING

Time of Reading 11:40 to 12:40 P.M. New York, N.Y.

GC: You will have before you all the information that has been given in psychic readings by Edgar Cayce concerning communication with those who have passed into the spirit plane. You will correlate all of this information in a systematic way and manner, that this may be understood by the conscious mind of any individual studying the subject, and you will answer all questions that I will ask you concerning this subject that should be answered. You will continue with such information which was begun yesterday, March 16, 1927, in 5756-3.

EC: (After having the first suggestion repeated and being told to continue) Yes.

Now, we have the information here, and that as has been given.

Continuing:

First, let it be understood there is the pattern in the material or physical plane of every condition as exists in the cosmic or spiritual plane, for things spiritual and things material are but those same conditions raised to a different condition of the same element—for all force is as of one force.

In that period when the spirit, or when the soul, (best that these be classified, that these be not misunderstood, then, in their relations one to another) is in the material, the body physically composed of the physical body, the mind, and the soul, add the subconscious mind, and the superconscious mind, or the spirit.

In the make-up of the active forces of the physical body, it (the body) is constituted of many, many, cells—each with its individual world within itself, controlled by the spirit that is everlasting, and guided by that of the soul, which is a counterpart—or the breath that makes that body individual, and when the body is changed, and this is the soul body, the elements as are patterned are of the same.

That is, that builded by thought and deed becomes the active particles, atoms, that make up that soul body, see?

When the soul passes, then, from the physical body, it (the soul body) then constituted with those atoms of thought (that are mind) and are of the Creative Forces a part, and then we have the soul body, with the mind, the subconscious mind, its attributes—which have been explained or given heretofore, as the relation of what the subconscious mind is— which never forgets, and is then as the sensuous [conscious] mind of the soul body; the spirit or superconscious mind being that as the subconscious mind of the material body—the place, then, of the resident or residence, or that occupied by the soul body becomes to the finite mind the first question. The occupancy is at once—as is seen here, there are about us many, *many*, many, soul bodies; those upon whom the thought of an individual, the whole being of an individual is attracted to, by that element of thought—just the same as the action in the material body—for remember, we are patterned, see? one as of another. In the next, then, we find that, that as *builded* by that soul is as the residence of that soul, the companion with that as has been builded by that soul— either of the earthbound or of that element or sphere, or plane, that has its attraction through that created in that soul being in the actions, by the thoughts, of that as an individual. Hence we find there are presented the same conditions in the astral or cosmic world, or cosmic consciousness, as is present in the material plane—until the consciousness of that soul has reached that development wherein such a soul is raised to that consciousness *above* the earth's sphere, or earth's attractive forces—until it reaches up, up, outward, until included in the *all*, see?

In the next step, then, we find, as regarding information given, the ability of such a body, or entity, to communicate with those in the material plane:

Question and answers are often confusing, by those that give or supply information concerning such experiences; for each experience is as individual as the individual that receives same, or the entity that transmits same, and the possibility, probability, the *ability*, of individuals to so communicate, or so draw on those forces, is raised, limited, or gained, by the act of the individual seeking its ability to so communicate—for, remembering, conditions are not changed. We find individuals at times communicative. At other times uncommunicative. There are moods, and there are moods. There are conditions in which such conditions are easily attained. There are others that are hard, as it were, to meet or cope with. The same condition remains in that distant sphere—as is felt by many—when it is the *same* sphere, *unless* the individual, or the entity, has passed on.

Then the next question that arises is: How are such communications brought about? Just as given. When the body (material) attunes self to that plane wherein the sensuous consciousness is in obeisance to the laws of physical or material, and the spiritual or astral laws are effective, those of the astral plane may communicate, in thought, in power, in form. What form, then, do such bodies assume? The desired form as is built and made by that individual in its experience through the material plane. Remembering our pattern. We find bodies are made by the action of cell units in the material body. Some to beauty, some to distress by that merited for the physical experience. Hence a necessity of a physical experience, that the *desires* that build may be made, changed, or acted upon.

Again we return to the astral or the soul body. In the various forms of communication, why, *why*, is such communication so often of seemingly an unnecessary nature, or seemingly inadequate to the mind of the soul entity, as understood by the mind of one hearing, seeing, or experiencing, such a communication? As may be illustrated in: The message as may be received from the boy just passed into the spirit world, and able through mediumistic forces of someone to communicate to mother, "All is well. Do not grieve. Do not long for the change." Such seems to be in the nature of rebuke to a sensuous mind when momentous questions as might be propounded, could be, or would be—as some mind would say—given. Remember the pattern as is set before. Is the greeting, *is* the greeting of some profound questions the first meeting? Rather cultivate that of such communications, and receive the answer to that of the most profound that may be propounded in any way and manner to those seeking such information. Is such information always true? Always true, so far as the individual has brought self into that attunement as is necessary for the perfect understanding of same. Do not attempt to govern information, or judge information, by the incorrect law, see? When force is taken, what is the impelling force such as is seen in the movement of material objects? When under stress, the communication or the appearance of the soul body is in contact with the individual mind; such as we have seen and experienced through that of the information as has been given. Such impelling forces, we find, are the combination of that in the individual receiving and in the abilities of the individual so communicating—that is, we find that in the various experiences of individuals, levitation, or

objects that are of material nature, are moved about by the active principle of the *individual through whom such manifestations are being made*, and
not by spirit action, or soul action. Yet *controlled* by that cosmic consciousness. Don't leave that out, see? Controlled—for, as given, the body
must be subjugated that such force may manifest. Then we see undue
strength, undue power, is seen exercised at such periods. True—for things
that are controlled by spirit alone are of a great deal greater active force
than of the sensuous mind, as a trained mind is more active than one
untrained.

Now many questions have been given. Many various forms of the
active forces of communicative energies, or of soul forces, as are manifested in the spirit world and in the material world, have been given—
but these as we have given here are set forth that those who would
study may have the basis of an understanding that will give each and
everyone that knowledge that the physical world, and the cosmic world,
or the astral world, are one—for the consciousness, the sensuous–consciousness, is as the growth from the subconsciousness into the material world. The growth in the astral world is the growth, or the digesting
and the building of that same oneness in the spirit, the conscious, the
subconscious, the cosmic, or the astral world. We find, from one to another, individuals—individuals—retained in that oneness, until each is
made one in the Great Whole—the Creative Energy of the Universal
Forces as are ever manifest in the material plane.

We are ready for the questions that may be asked, as we see here,
concerning various conditions—for many are gathered about to give
their various experiences as have been passed through in this transition
period.

(Q) *Is it possible for those that have passed into the spirit plane to at all times
communicate with those in the earth plane?*

(A) Yes and no—for these conditions are as has been described—that
the *necessary* way or mode must be prepared; for as this: Ever has that
vibration as is attracted and thrown off been active in the world as is
exercised through that called the telephone, but without proper connection, without shorts, without any disturbance, may proper communication be made! These have not always been active to the *physical*
body. These are not always in proper accord to be used by the physical

body. Just the same in that pattern. Those in the astral plane are not always ready. Those in the physical plane are not always ready. What conditions arise (is asked) that we in the physical plane are not ready? The *mind!* What conditions arise that we in the astral plane are not ready? There are those same elements as has been outlined, of that of the development going on, and the willingness of that *individual* to communicate, as given, see? but when set aright, these may—until passed into that Oneness, or returned again, or gone on beyond such communications.

(Q) *What physical thing may an individual do to be able to communicate with those that have passed into the spirit plane?*

(A) Lay aside the carnal or sensuous mind and desire that those who would use that mentality, that soul, for its vehicle of expression, do so in the manner chosen by that soul; for some communicate in act, in sight, in movement, in voice, in writing, in drawing, in speaking, and in the various forces as are manifest—for force is *one* force.

(Q) *What form or body does the spirit entity assume upon leaving the earth or material body?*

(A) Just as given. That builded by the body in its experience. We illustrate: Would one of a uniform body desire a change—would one of a crippled body desire a change the answer, as has oft been given: *Act* that way, *it*—the result, the change—comes about.

(Q) *Where is the dwelling place of such spirit entities?*

(A) That that such entity has builded, and as it (the entity) draws about it, or desires same shall be. In the earth's plane many are attracted by those conditions and are held by many loved ones, when their desires to be on the way, as it were. Building in that way and manner as is in its heart of hearts, soul of soul, to be about. See? Now, the dwelling place is as builded by that entity, and in that place about the earth and the earth's sphere, time is no time, space no space, to such entities.

(Q) *Is the effort for spirit communication as much effort on the part of the spirit entity as the effort that should be made on the part of the material or physical entity?*

(A) The force should never be applied, and may never be applied and be real, in either case. The willingness and the desire from both is necessary for the perfect communication, see? Illustrate this same condition by that physical condition as is seen in attunement of either that called radio, or of that called phone, or that of any of that vibratory force as is set by the electron in the material plane. Necessary for the perfect union that each be in accord. In other words, we find many in the astral plane *seeking* to give force active in the material. Many in the material *seeking* to delve into the astral. They must be made one, would they bring the better.

(Q) *What form of consciousness does the spirit entity assume?*

(A) That of the subconscious consciousness, as known in the material plane, or the acts and deeds, and thoughts, done in the body, are ever present before that being. Then consider what a hell digged by some, and what a haven and heaven builded by many.

(Q) *What are the powers of the spirit entity?*

(A) Raised to the highest power as is developed in that plane, and are—as outlined—as *varying* as individual's power or ability to manifest, or to exercise that manifestation, in the material. We have not changed, see? for as we would say: What is the power of an individual in the *physical* plane? Naught as it enters. Naught until it reaches that ability to *give* of self in service. Yet, as we find, there is in all the world nothing that offers so much possibility as when the body of the human is born into the material plane. In the minds of every other, nothing offers more beautiful condition, raised to its same power, as the birth into that of the astral plane. Hence, how oft, how oft, is such seen in this entering! How expectant becomes both? Does it become a wonder at that vision as Stephen sees, when "My Lord, standing ready to *receive* me," see?

(Q) *Is it possible for those passing into the spiritual plane to be conscious of both the material and the spiritual plane?*

(A) Just as given. Just as is seen in the various experiences of those who are spiritually minded—yet many carnal minds have passed from the body for days before they realized they were passed. Sensuousness!

(Q) *Describe to me what (Mrs. [3776]) saw as she entered the spirit plane, when she said "Mrs. [139] says she will guide me over."*

(A) Just that same experience as has just been described. The desire in the mind—soul mind—and the physical mind, to be at a oneness, one with the other, and to give to each that as necessary for that wonderful development possible in that plane—for, as is seen, we find as this experience in *this* condition: The mind in that accord with the soul forces, in action, meets those who are the active in that of the aid in the development. Hence we find this very active force in the soul body, Mrs. [139] ready—and with that consciousness of the conditions in action going on—guiding and meeting the soul body in its transition, and the spirit body, mind, soul, attuned in that of the physical body, (Mrs. [3776]), so it answers one with another, and is capable of being hearkened back or to such condition, see?

(Q) How may force act in unmaterialized form—i.e. without matter to embrace in itself the many individual self consciousness separated by space in the material form—i.e. man, but all one inner self in the cosmic or 4th dimension?

(A) Just in the manner as has been described and given, in how that the transition of one force becomes as the portion of the whole force. As is, that each is the pattern, one of another, or as may be illustrated: How does the force or power transmitted from the powerhouse light each individual globe in the city? Each have their connection. Each have their various forms, or their various powers, according to that as has been set. Now, applying same in the illustrative forces, we find each being in accord, each being in the direct connection, each apply, manifest, according to that as is builded in the individual in its transition, or in its experience, and as the various forces are manifested each give off that as is taken on.

We are through for the present.

Reading 900-330

(Q) In regard to the educational work in my connection with the Association, I am now entering upon that phase of the phenomena called Spirit Communication. I have experienced this myself quite frequently of late, in a very natural and pronounced manner. Will you give any special kind of reading that I may ask for in relation to these particular and personal experiences?

(A) As has been given as respecting spirit communication, these are of the individual nature, and are of rather the individual interpretation, and when such are presented through, of, for, or on any other way or manner, there may be the suspect of there entering in other force than that of individual importance of individual understanding.

In the matter of spirit communication:

As is seen, as has been given, there are ever about those in the flesh in the earth's plane those desiring to communicate with those in the earth plane, attracted by the act, intent and purport of the individual, or by the act, intent, purport, of that entity in the spirit plane.

In these as have been, as are being presented to this body, [900], these are above the ordinary experiences, and are of the definite position, condition, and represent definite phases in the understanding of the entity.

Study same, then, with that same knowledge as was given of old, that God the Father speaks to Himself through man and man's activities in the earth. The spirit is of the Father, and all force is of God. Study these from this phase. As to information concerning definite or specific instances of communication, these may receive—through these sources—the interpretation, either of the giver, or of those associated in the spirit plane with such entities, see? for various phases of such communication present themselves much as the various phases of the development of entities, and those intents, those purports as were once set forth by Saul of Tarsus, are as near the correct interpretation of spirit communication as may be attained in any literature or writings that may be attained at the present period.

Prepare that thou art preparing concerning such conditions, and these will equal—or even be better understood than that as was given by him in those passages concerning the gifts of the spirit. Read same.

(Q) *What part of the Bible?*

(A) Paul—in the Epistle to the Corinthians.

Reading 900-363

That of the correct understanding will give the better understanding of spirit communication, or the activity of the forces from cosmic plane activity in the material forces; remembering, then, first there must be proper attunement for the correct understanding of *any* condition presented to a sensuous mind. From the present then, we find that given of "Seek and ye shall find," in its broaden sense is answered in that experienced here. That is, when self desires—and puts desire in action, with self in attunement in the spiritual sense—that same reasoning as spoken of self's subconscious self gives answer from within, and accorded to by cosmic forces in attunement with that desired. Hence the feeling of innate action separated from cosmic forces, or urge, or push. This then gives one the understanding that though there may be many urges from without and within, unless self has lost through inactivity the power of self, then self's action accorded by will is ever the stronger force, whether related to those urges from the physical surroundings and all its elements of urge, or from spiritual surroundings with its urge from developed or from cosmic entities' action on same; for self remains ever the portion of the whole, irrespective of those elements that have to do with either the mental materialness or the spiritual activity actualities of that plane. Hence like begets like, and man—or the *being* itself—is the pilot, director and keeper of self.

8

●

Cayce on Higher Consciousness

Editor's Note: The following readings give insight into the nature of consciousness and the higher levels of consciousness from Cayce's unique perspective.

Text of Reading 826-11 M 36
(Lawyer, Protestant)

This psychic reading given by Edgar Cayce at his home on Arctic Crescent, Virginia Beach, Va., this 11th day of January, 1938, in accordance with request made by self—Mr. [826], Active Member of the Ass'n for Research & Enlightenment, Inc.

PRESENT

Edgar Cayce; Gertrude Cayce, Conductor; Gladys Davis, Steno. Mr. [826] and Hugh Lynn Cayce.

READING

Time of Reading 11:00 to 11:55 A.M. Eastern Standard Time. Washington, D.C.

(Entity, who seeks a Mental and Spiritual Reading with reference to his soul development and purpose for entrance into the earth plane during this age; also who seeks information, advice and guidance as to how he may carry out this purpose in practical application for the benefit of mankind. You will answer the questions he submits, as I ask them, regarding information which has been given him through this channel—and its application.)

EC: Yes, we have the entity here, [826]; with the abilities physical and mental, and the use or application of same as has been made by the entity in its experiences or sojourns in the earth—all of which become a part of the entity in the present.

In giving that as we find that may be helpful to this entity, first the purposes for which an entity enters a material experience—and why:

In giving such there must be given then some premise that is acceptable or stated as being a practical thing or condition in the experience of the entity; that it may be a part of the entity in fulfilling that purpose in the present experience.

The entity or man then is physical, mental and spiritual; or the physical body, the mental body, the spiritual body.

The spiritual is that portion of same, or that body, that is everlasting; that is a portion of all it has applied in its mental experiences through the sojourns in the environs of which the entity or soul or spirit body is a part.

From whence came then this spirit body, that we find in consciousness in the present; aware of the physical attributes, aware of at least a portion of its mental abilities, its mental capacities; only catching a glimpse here and there in the application of spiritual laws or spiritual truths of the spiritual body?

The spirit is the universal consciousness, or God; that which is the First Cause; that which is manifested in all the varied forms and manners that are experienced in the activities of the individual in this particular sphere of activity or phase of consciousness in the present.

Why the entity—why the spirit of this entity? A gift, a companion—yea, a very portion of that First Cause.

Hence the purposes that it, the entity, the spirit body, may make manifest in materiality or in physical consciousness the more and more awareness of the relationships of the mental body, the physical body to eternity, infinity, or the God-Consciousness.

Why? That is the purpose, that is the gift, that is the activity for maintaining its consciousness throughout matter, mind or spirit.

For, as is the consciousness of the entity in materiality, when there is such a diffusion of consciousness as to change, alter or create a direction for an activity of any influence that has taken on consciousness of matter to waver it from its purpose for being in a consciousness, it loses its individual identity.

What then is the purpose of the entity's activity in the consciousness of mind, matter, spirit in the present?

That it, the entity, may *know* itself to *be* itself and part of the Whole; not the Whole but one *with* the whole; and thus retaining its individuality, knowing itself to be itself yet one with the purposes if the First Cause that called it, the entity, into *being*, into the awareness, into the consciousness of itself.

That is the purpose, that is the cause of *being*.

Then the natural question to the entity becomes, "What may I do about same? In what manner, in what way may I apply myself as an entity, as an individual, to fill that purpose whereunto the First Cause has its influence, its way, its purpose with me?"

In such an activity then the body–physical, the body–mind, must be taken into consideration; with its faults, its fancies, its faith, its purpose, its abilities in every manner, and in every influence that has been and is a part of that mental or spiritual or material consciousness.

It has been given the entity as to much which or unto it may attain; as each entity bears an influence into and unto the Whole, and is influenced by same according to the will and purpose of the entity in the individual or the moment's expression.

For the choices are continually being made by the body, the mind, *upon* those things that are within *themselves* taken within the consciousness, the awareness of the entity.

Not that there are not *other* influences also that are aware only to the higher portion of the mental and spiritual self. For in the *body* few are aware of even the heartbeat, the fact of assimilation, the fact of distribution, the fact of building or of degeneration.

In the purpose then or premise; it is that:

Mind is the Builder, being both the spiritual and material; and the consciousness of same reaches man only in his awareness of his consciousness through the senses of his physical being.

Then indeed do the senses take *on* an activity in which they may be directed in that awareness, that consciousness of the spiritual self as well as in the physical indulgences or appetites or activities that become as a portion of the selfish nature of the individual or entity.

It behooves the entity first in its premise then to know, to conceive, to imagine, to become aware of that which is its ideal.

Not that alone of the ideal condition of the body as in relationship to its appetites, its factors—yea, even its functionings, nor only the abilities of the mind to be in the physical manner directed in such a way or manner that it may bring that which is the answer to the desires of the flesh. But also, or *rather*, that which takes hold on those things that are eternal in not *only* their awareness, not only in their application but in their body, yea in their mind, yea in their application!

For as is the awareness of the mental self, the Spirit of God—or Good—is never seen by the material man, ever; only the effects and the application of those factors in the experience of the individual are made aware by that it brings into the consciousness through the senses,—yea of the body, the awareness of the mental self and the spiritual self.

And this kept as a part of the development, the growth, the activity of the entity as a whole, becomes then a well- balanced unit; an entity that *is* conscious of the influences of infinity through the finite forces that may be given in what has been expressed as of old, "As ye do it unto the least of these thy brethren, ye do it unto thy Maker."

How, then, may an entity become aware of those influences of that infinite force and power, and intelligence that is the ruling force of that ideal life as may be manifested by this entity in this individual experience?

When the mental self is loosened in the quietness of those periods when it would take cognizance of the influences about self, we find the mental as a vapor, as a gas (not that it is either, but as comparison) is loosened by the opening of the self through those centers of the body that arouse the awareness of the mental to the indwelling of the spiritual self that is a portion of and encased within self. And it, the energy, the influence—as the vapor, as the gas—rises to the consciousness within, to the temple of the motivative forces of the physical body.

It, that energy, seeks—by the natural law—that to which it has an affinity. Affinity is the ideal, then.

If that mental self, that portion of the Spirit is in accord with the Divine Will—by its application of its knowledge as to its relationships to the fellow man in the manners and purposes as indicated—there comes that consciousness, that awareness that His Spirit indeed beareth witness with thy spirit.

And indeed ye may then find that access, that consciousness of His abiding presence with thee that ye may carry on, ye may fulfill, ye may keep inviolate all promises that thou hast made to thy Maker; that He hath made to thee!

Thus it is through thine own self. For indeed thy body is the temple of the living God. It is the temple of thine own awareness. It is the temple of thine own conscious walk with Him.

And the application of that received there, then, in the physical consciousness, physical mind—applied in thy relationships to those ye meet day by day—causes the growth to come.

Even as in or within thine own body ye become in body a part of that ye digest within thine own physical self.

Thus only that ye digest within thine own spiritual body may ye apply in the building up of the mental and spiritual self for that activity in the *eternal* consciousness of the Father-God.

So, keep thy physical body inviolate, in such an active way and manner that it may become more and more aware of this indwelling consciousness that may give to thy mind, as a whole, as an entity, the *best* tools to work with.

For if the body is racked with doubts—by the use of those influences in same that have set at naught this continuous effort of same to assimilate and distribute for activity in its own physical self—it becomes unfit for the duties, the obligations—yea the beauties, yea the *opportunities* of itself in its associations with those of its fellow centers, its fellow activities; or energies that are—each in its atomic self—a portion of the whole.

Keep the body-physical, then, well-balanced in those infusions of what? that are as energies that are positive and negative forces within the material activity, known or classed as the proper chemical balance in same—the fusion of the activities from the material angles that are acid and alkaline; also the potash and activities in its forces that become the making of materiality by the activity of mind upon same in its influence in the physical forces of self.

Hence in these manners may the entity, as a physical being, as a mental being, dwell upon the things not alone of the physical being but upon the spiritual, the things that are eternal; that it, too, may be kept in a balance such as that thy good may not be evil-spoken of, that thy evil may not become so overbalanced as to wreck thine *own* self in its influences and its activities in thy conscious walk among thy fellow man.

These meditated upon then, these kept in the ways that ye know. It is not then that ye *know* as a physical consciousness, but that ye *apply* of good, of that which *is* of God, that makes ye know that consciousness of His walks with thee.

For thy physical self may only see the reflection of good, while thy spiritual self may *be* that good in the activities of thy fellow man in such measures that ye bring—what?

Ever, *ever*, the fruits of the Spirit in their awareness; longsuffering, brotherly love, patience, kindness, gentleness, *hope* and faith!

If ye in thy activities in any manner with thy fellow man destroy these in the minds, in the heart of thy fellow man, ye are not only slipping but ye have taken hold on the path of destruction.

Then so love, so act, so *think* that others *seeing* thy good works, thy hopes that ye bring, thy faith that ye manifest, thy patience that ye show, may *also* glorify Him.

For that cause, for that purpose ye entered into the materiality in the present.

To what, ye ask, may ye attain—and how may ye attain same?

That is only limited by thyself. For He, the Father-God, loveth all alike; but that ye find within thy mind, thy body, that would offend, pluck it away! For thy will as one with His may do *all* these things in *His* name!

Then, to what heights may ye attain? That height to which thy consciousness is ever clear before the throne of thy awareness with Him; which is to know the glory of the Father through thy dealings with thy fellow man; which is to know—no sin, no sorrow, no disappointments in him. Oft is He disappointed in thee, but if thou dost bring such into the minds, the hearts, the lives of others, what is thy reflection but these same experiences?

But to love good, to flee from veil, to bring the awareness of the God-Consciousness into the minds and hearts of others is *thy* purpose in this experience.

Ready for questions.

(Q) *Is there any particular psychic faculty which I should develop in this experience that would enrich my daily life?*

(A) As has been indicated, this may be developed in the manner as has been given. It is the heritage of each soul. If ye in thine own consciousness are desirous of meeting Him, thy Maker, thy Father in the temple of thine own soul, then meditate upon Him, applying that ye know today!

For it is in the application, not the knowledge, that the truth becomes a part of thee.

It is not in thine body that what ye eat is thy body, but that the body—through thy digestive self—puts *into use in* muscle, bone, blood, tissue,—yea the very blood and the very streams thorough which the mentality flows! Thy *brain* is not thy mind, it is that which is used by thy mind!

What then *is* thy mind? The gift of God, that is the companion with thy soul, that is a part of same! Then if ye would develop that by its use, by its application, it is ministering good and goodness; not for self. For that ye give away *alone* do ye possess! For the that would have life must give it. He that would know the faculties of the psychic force, or the soul, must *manifest* same in the relationships to spiritual truths, spiritual law, spiritual application.

(Q) *Please explain in detail the steps I should take in this development, in meditation, that would be most consistent with my inner self?*

(A) In whatever manner that thine own consciousness is a cleansing of the body and of the mind, that ye may present thyself *clean* before thyself and before thy God, *do*! Whether washing of the body with water, purging of same with oils, or surrounding same with music or incense. But *do that thy consciousness* directs thee! Not questioning! For he that doubteth has already built his barrier!

Then, meditation upon that which is thy highest ideal within thyself, raise the vibrations from thy lower self, thy lower consciousness through the centers of thy body to the temple of thy mind, thy brain, thy eye that is single in purpose; or to the glandular forces of the body as the Single Eye.

Then, listen—listen! For it is not in the storm, not in the noise, but the still small voice that rises within.

And let thy query ever be:

Here am I, O God, use me—send me! Do with me as Thou seest! Not my will, but Thine—O God—be done in and through me.

These are the manners. Not that the things of the material mind are to be neglected, but remember this: It is the foolishness of God that is the wisdom of man. It is the wisdom of man misapplied that is the foolishness to God.

(Q) How may I come to a greater realization of my inner spiritual power and the relation of this power to all Creative Force?

(A) That has been given over and over again, here in this: In *applying* that ye know *today*! and tomorrow the next step is given. For it is line upon line, precept upon precept, here a little, there a little. And if ye would have thy God,—yea thy better self be patient with thee, then be patient with thy study, yea thy fellow man.

For indeed as He gave, "In patience possess ye your souls."

Then, as ye are manifested before thy consciousness *in* thy consciousness, become aware of this; not only as ye see the unfoldment of life in matter as a manifestation of that force and power ye would worship as thy God, thy companion, thy Lord, yea thy *brother*, thy portion of thyself, *but* in time, in space, in patience is the heart of it all!

We are through for the present.

Text of Reading 601-11 F 50
(Housewife, Jewish)

This psychic reading given by Edgar Cayce at his home on Arctic Crescent, Virginia Beach, Va., this 17th day of January, 1936, in accordance with request made by the self—Mrs. [601], Active Member of the Ass'n for Research & Enlightenment, Inc.

PRESENT

Edgar Cayce; Gertrude Cayce, Conductor; Gladys Davis, Steno. Hugh Lynn Cayce.

READING

Time of Reading 3:35 to 4:15 P.M. Eastern Standard Time. Detroit, Mich.

(Entity. You will give for this entity a mental and spiritual reading, giving the reason for the entrance into this solar cycle, and particularly stressing the directions for the highest proper development and expression in this earth's plane. You will answer the questions which she has submitted, as I ask them, regarding her mental and spiritual development through present associations.)

EC: There's always so much more about an entity than may be at all times interpreted.

We have the entity here, [601].

In giving the mental and spiritual influences and forces, and purposes for which the entity entered the present experience in this particular solar system, there are many things, many conditions, that are hard at times to be put into words; and that those who are of the material-minded manner fail to comprehend or to understand.

While the body is made up of the three divisions; body, mind and spirit—they are one. Yet each interpretation and each application of self, of the entity, of the mental and soul mind, to its experiences in the earth, are *just* as separate or distinct as may be the application of the *body* to the elements in the earth. *earth, air, fire, water*—these are one, in their *varied* aspects, to human or bodily existence; and are each necessary.

So are the experiences of an entity in entering the sphere or consciousness of activity for the meeting of those experiences of self in its relationship to universal or cosmic or God-consciousness in that particular phase of experience.

Just as a treatment for a body over-exposed or underexposed to water or fire would not meet same in materiality in the same manner.

Thus may the varied experiences of an entity in its sojourns through the earth, or through the varied consciousnesses of its activity, be met according to a first law, a first principle:

"Know, O Israel, the Lord thy God is *one!*"

All power, all force, is a manifestation of that which is termed the God-consciousness.

These are elemental or first statements, first principles.

Then, the application of an entity in materiality, is that of the first and the last law:

"Love the Lord thy God with all thy heart, thy mind, thy soul—*and* thy neighbor as thyself."

Then, each appearance, each application of an entity to those first principles, first laws in its experiences through the earth, is for the purpose that it may be completed in that as given, "The Lord hath not *willed* that any soul should perish, but hath with every temptation prepared a means, a way, of escape."

Then, for that purpose, for that activity, for that application of these laws, these principles, these causes in the experience of each soul, does each soul enter. For this is *its* purpose, *the* purpose, for the entering into material or solar or earth's manifestation at *any* time.

For in the earth or the earth's dimensional experience one becomes (an entity, a soul becomes) aware that there are three phases of its being; body, mind, soul—yet all in one. Just as the laws—as those given—are One.

So, the activities of an entity into the earth are to meet *self* and make the application of the love of the Father as it would to itself, in the sons of men; that the glory of the Lord may encompass the earth—even to become His holy dwelling place.

This is the purpose of *this* entity's sojourn; *this* entity's activity.

How, then, may the entity—with the knowledge *of* its own self's activities in the earth, through its varied experiences in same—go about to apply same, to become more and more aware of its at–oneness, its consciousness *of* its at–oneness with that consciousness of *being* one with this applied law, this applied love in its experience?

As has been given, "Do that thou *knowest* to *do today*, and *then* the next step may be given thee."

For ye know that ye are studying to show self approved unto that consciousness, that awareness, and are keeping self unspotted from that *thou* knowest that might, would or could, cause thy brother to be offended. And ye come more and more, by such living, to the awareness of His presence abiding with thee! Not unto vainglorying, not unto self–consciousness; but rather that "Here am I, Lord, use me. Let *me* be that channel of blessing to *someone today*; that Thy love, Thy glory, Thy oneness, may be the greater manifested in not only my experience but those that I contact day by day."

Reading 2109–2

(Q) Did I have the experience called illumination or cosmic consciousness, in this incarnation?

(A) As indicated,—how oft has remaining quiet aided thee in seeing and feeling and experiencing the full cosmic consciousness! Yes!

This is found, as has been the experience, by the opening of those channels within the physical body through which the energies of the Infinite are attuned to the centers through which physical consciousness, mental activity, is attained,—or in deep meditation.

(Q) Can I help [2156]? How?

(A) By the awareness of calling upon the universal consciousness to be in accord with that which may bring the better forces into the experience of [2156].

Text of Reading 272-9 F 37
(Schoolteacher, Protestant)

This psychic reading given by Edgar Cayce at his home on Arctic Crescent, Virginia Beach, Virginia, this 31st day of August, 1935, in accordance with request made by the self— Mrs. [272], Active Member of the Ass'n for Research & Enlightenment, Inc.

PRESENT

Edgar Cayce; Gertrude Cayce, Conductor; Gladys Davis, Steno. L.B. Cayce.

READING

Time of Reading 11:00 to 11:45 A.M. Eastern Standard Time . . . , Alabama.

(Entity, who seeks that needed at this time to enable her to reach the Christ Consciousness. You will answer the questions she has submitted, as I ask them.)

EC: Yes, we have the enquiring mind, [272]; those desires, those abilities, those weaknesses, those strengths that are as a portion of the entity at the present time.

In seeking that which may be helpful to the body–mind and body–consciousness in the present, well that the entity review in part much that has been given and that has been learned by the body.

The man, the body, and the manifestations of the flesh are as but a channel, a manner, a means through which the soul may through its activities manifest the attributes of the spirit of truth. Man finds himself in that state where he is subject to the faults, the failures, those conditions that work upon the weaknesses wherein he has failed. And, as an individual finds, these work through environmental and hereditary influences, also through associations. Yet there is ever the awareness in the experiences of those who seek, that the Father, the God, the Creative Force, has prepared—has given man, the individual—the way of escape from those things that so easily beset. That the activities must become the voluntary choice of the entity, the soul, has been shown, manifested, given in the manner in which the Christ Consciousness in the earth was manifested through the lowly Nazarene; that came in order that man—through His example, His love, His patience, His hope manifested, through the attributes of the Spirit that He exemplified in His activity both as to word and as to precept—might choose, as He, to do that which is right, that which is just, that which is sincere, that which is honest in the activities one with another. And as He has given, "As ye do it unto the least of thy brethren, ye do it unto me."

Also He has given, as the Father's promise has been to Him and to man through those various channels of approach, "Ye abiding in me and I in the Father, ye may know that consciousness that I and the Father abide in thee." That is the manner in which the individual, the soul, may at *this* time become more and more aware of the Christ Consciousness, that manifested by and through the man Jesus, that is the promise and the sureness as shown in Him from the Father unto thee.

The way is simple. Yet those who would seek through the mysteries of nature, the mysteries of the manifestations of life in the earth, or those who would see rather the activities of their neighbors, friends, associates day by day, than listen to that which may be had through the still small voice from within, become in the position of being troubled and wondering—and then fearful; and then there come those periods when the sureness of self is lacking.

All things having force or power in the earth, in the heavens, in the sea, are given that power from Him; that those who seek may know Him the better. He hath not willed, He hath not destined that any soul should perish. In patience, in persistency, in consistency of thy manifestations of His love before and to and of thy fellow man, ye become aware that thy soul is a portion of the Creator, that it is the gift of the Father *to thee*. This is manifested in thine daily experience. That portion of thy body which is of the earth-earthy remains with the earth, but that thou hast glorified, that thou hast used as a channel for the manifestations of His Spirit—of thy soul in communion with Him, *that* body will be raised with Him in righteousness. That the physical body becomes ensnared, entangled in those things in the earth, through the gratifying of those desires that are fleshly alone, those that are carnal, is manifested by the dis-ease, the corruption, the turmoil, the strife that arises within the experience of each soul in its *thoughtful* activities in the earth.

The soul, then, must return—*will* return—to its Maker. It is a portion of the Creative Force, which is energized into activity even in materiality, in the flesh. Yet it may, with thine own understanding and thine own manifestations, come to be as a portion of that thou bringest in thy love into thy fellow man, for thy Father-God, for thy activity to be *one* with Him in those realms of activity and experience that ye *are* aware of His presence, of His abiding love, of His abiding faith *in* thee motivating thee in thy activities in every direction.

Then, just being kind, just being patient, just showing love for thy
fellow man; *that* is the manner in which an individual works *at* becoming aware of the consciousness of the Christ Spirit.

He hath given that where the treasure is, where the heart is, *there*
doth the soul make manifest the greater glorious activities that make
for the growth through the mind, the body; the soul becomes aware of
that sphere of activity, that growth whereunto there has become the
experience of His abiding presence ever.

In a material expression—as thou hast seen in thine own activities
among thine counsels, among thine helps to those that seek the material things of life—how, when and in what way does an individual become aware of the laws pertaining to the construction of a sentence in
English? How, where, when, in what manner does an individual learn
the rule of spelling a word? By the meditating upon same, by seeing,
visualizing, acting. And then the *awareness* of same is manifested by the
manner in which the individual puts same into practice in conjunction
or association with its fellow man. The knowledge may be existent, the
awareness in self may be present; but if the individual does not apply
same in its associations—or if it uses some other manner, some other
way of expression than that it has set as the rule or the standard—it
becomes of none effect.

What are the rules, then? As has just been outlined, ye may become
aware of His presence abiding with thee. When ye manifest love, patience, hope, charity, tolerance, faith; these be the manners. Not in thine
own *self!* These as words, these as expressions, these as visualized *objects*
may be within thine self. But when ye as a soul, as an entity, as an
individual, make such manifest to those ye meet casually, to those that
ye contact day by day—in conversation, in example, in precept; these
the attributes of the Spirit—ye become aware of that Consciousness, of
that Christ Spirit, of that Christ Consciousness as He gave, "Ye abiding in
me and I in the Father, we—the Father, I will *come* and abide with thee."

When the Spirit of the Father, when the activities that the Christ—the
man—gave to the sons of men—are made manifest in thine own life day
by day, then ye become aware of His presence abiding in thee.

Know the Truth, for the truth is as He gave; the truth is He, and His words. For He hath given, "Though the heavens and the earth may pass away, *my* words, my promise, shall *not* pass away."

Let not, then, the cares of the world, the deceitfulness of riches, the pomp and glory of the earthly nature, or fame or even to be well-spoken of, hinder thee from *applying* in thy relationships with thy fellow man that thou *knowest* to be

the manner in which ye may become aware of His presence.

That offenses must come is true. But woe to him that bringeth same to pass!

Then, be not idle in that ye know; rather let it be an *active, positive* influence in the experience of all. Let love be without dissimulation. Abhor that which is evil, cleave to that which is good.

In *this* way may *ye* know, may *ye* be aware of His presence within thee.

Just as thou hast seen in thine own body that which has brought the fires of nature, the turmoils of dis-ease, the wonderments even of distress. Yet ye have seen those influences, those powers in nature that are manifestations of His love to man, so that—when ye have fallen away, and into those things that *bring* such hindrances in thine life and thine experience—the *Way* is prepared. *Whose* way? Who hath prepared the Way? Man in *any* phase of his experience is but the channel to make application, or to give that which may be a helpful understanding; he is but being used as a channel. Even as *thou* may be, to make for the awareness in the experiences of others of His abiding presence being in and with thee!

Ready for questions.

(Q) May the vibrations of my body be raised to that which will bring purity and a normal functioning of all its organs?

(A) Apply in their regular order, in decency and in order, in love and in patience, those things that have been given thee as to the manner of expression; cleansing thine body in the ways and manners as thou hast seen, as thou hast known, as thou may comprehend more and more, would make thee as one set apart, as one dedicating its abilities of every nature to the service of the fellow man. Thus may that service bring to thee the awareness of *His* force, *His* power, working in and through thy body. *Thus* may the vibrations be raised; *thus* may thy body be cleansed; thus may thy mind have the greater channel, the greater ways and means of manifesting that thou wouldst show forth in thine activities for thine greater, thine better understanding.

(Q) *Please give that which will be of help in my present development to attain the Christ Consciousness.*

(A) Applying that—*applying* that—which has been so oft given. Let love direct thee, with little thought of self; rather with the attitude that the Christ Love, the Christ Consciousness may be made manifest day by day.

(Q) *May I sit at the Master's feet and learn of Him?*

(A) Learn by applying His precepts, His life, in thine *own* relationship with thy fellow man.

How gave He when he was called and told that his mother and brethren waited without? "Who is my mother? Who is my brother, my sister? He that doeth the will of my Father." What is the will? "Love the Lord thy God with all thine mind, thy body, thy soul, and thy neighbor as thyself."

Who is thy neighbor? He that seeks to know more and more of the love of the Father through the Son.

Who is the Son? He that doeth the will of the Father, in *whatever* sphere of activity that may be.

(Q) *How could I improve my meditations?*

(A) By being, as given, more and more patient, more and more longsuffering, more and more tolerant, more and more *lovely* to everyone ye meet in *every* way ye act, in every word ye *speak*, in every thought ye think.

(Q) *Is it best that I marry again and may it be a spiritual marriage?*

(A) When there is the answer of the soul *to* another, *then* ye may seek, then ye may know, then ye may ask even of the Father and be *made* aware *of* that ye should do under such circumstance.

For the individual, the soul, may so live that the acts of the body, the thoughts of the mind, may be one with Him.

Let thy light so shine that others seeing thy light, thy life, may take hope. Be patient; be persistent; be consistent in what ye do, in what ye say.

We are through for the present.

Text of Reading 262-29

This psychic reading given by Edgar Cayce at his home on Arctic Crescent, Va. Beach, Va., this 2nd day of October, 1932, in accordance with request made by those present.

P R E S E N T

Edgar Cayce; Gertrude Cayce, Conductor; Gladys Davis, Steno. Minnie & C.A. Barrett, Esther Wynne, Hannah Miller, Florence & Edith Edmonds, F. Y. Morrow, L.B., H.L. & Annie Cayce, Mildred Davis, Helen Storey, Sarah Hesson, Helen Ellington, Ruth LeNoir, Katherine Zvirin, Evelyn D. Ott & husband, & other visitors.

R E A D I N G

Time of Reading 3:45 to 4:30 P.M.

GC: You will have before you the group gathered here and their work on the lesson *The Open Door*, a copy of which I hold in my hand. You will please give any suggestions as to changes or expansions in this data, and continue any further information on this subject which will aid us in preparing this lesson. You will answer the questions which individuals will ask:

EC: Yes, we have the group as gathered here, and their work in the preparation of the lesson *The Open Door*.

In that which has been so far prepared, it would be very well that this be continued in the same vein or manner, but expressed or given in the terms for the individual, or the individual interpretations, that this may reach in its entirety the greater numbers which has been indicated is necessary for the greater good to be accomplished through the distribution of such data that is presented in such lessons.

For those who have as yet not become contributors to this lesson, begin rather in the manner that has been indicated for each. How does cooperation make for an attribute to the open door? Cooperation, as has been indicated, is making self selfless in the way that the ideal of the body may be in that phase of experience as to be led by the Ideal; thus, when properly considered, becoming the opening of the door that

He who stands and knocks may enter in. In making self selfless selfishness is obliterated, that there may be the activity of the ideal, and being led then by the spirit of truth gains the understanding of the ideal in its operation upon the lives and activities of individuals; thus becoming a practical application in a material world through the spirit of truth that makes not afraid, but through faith leads on to the opening of the ways in virtue, understanding and patience, in which all become the more conscious of that oneness with the Father, so that as we are known of the Father so may we know the Father, thus making in the material activities of the mental and the conscious mind those channels that we as individuals, thus applying these necessary forces or activities in our own experience, become channels that the way may be known to others; thus entering into the kingdom of heaven.

This variation differentiates the kingdom of heaven from the kingdom of the Father: One is the experiences of the finite. The other is the glory with the Oneness in the infinite.

Thus, as individuals become aware of these activities, the kingdom of heaven is within. Even as He gave, not that this is to be attained only through transition; but through the consciousness, the awareness of the activity of the spirit of truth in and through us, as individuals, with that birthright of the sons of the Father; one with Him as the way, the truth, the light, that is shed abroad in the world, the earth, that we may have that advocate with the Father in light.

Ready for questions.

(Q) *What is meant by the throne of the Father?*

(A) The approach to being wholly in the at-oneness with the Father, reached only through the abilities to leave the carnal forces and be one in spirit with the Father.

(Q) *Please explain clearly the difference between the Christ Consciousness, the Christ Spirit.*

(A) As the difference might be given in that which makes for the birth in the flower, and the flower. The consciousness of the Spirit and the abilities to apply same are the differences in the Christ Consciousness, the Christ Spirit.

As has been given, the devils believe, the devils know, individuals that may be conscious of an activity. Those with the abilities to call upon, to be so unselfish as to allow the Spirit to operate in self's stead, are aware of the Spirit's activity, while those that may be conscious or aware of a truth may not wholly make it their own without that which has been given, "He that would have life must give life"; for *He* thought it not robbery to be equal with the Father, yet of Himself did nothing, "but the Father that worketh in me, through me."

Do thou likewise, that thou may know the consciousness of the Christ Spirit, and experience the operation of that witness, that "My Spirit beareth witness with thy spirit, that the Father may be glorified in you, even as I am glorified in the Father through you. If ye love me keep my commandments, and I will abide with you. I will *not* leave thee comfortless; I will make thee aware of that glory I possessed with the Father before the world was."

In such a manner may individuals become aware of the Christ Consciousness and become one with the operative forces of the Christ Spirit abroad in the earth; for He shall come again, even as ye have seen Him go. *Then* shall the Christ Spirit be manifest in the world, even as the Christ Consciousness may make thee aware of that promised as the Comforter in this material world.

Then, the Christ Consciousness is the Holy Spirit, or that as the promise of His presence made aware of His activity in the earth. The Spirit is as the Christ in action with the Spirit of the Father.

(Q) Explain and expand fully the thought that the Christ Spirit, not the man, should be the door, the truth, the way.

(A) That which has been given may be used to illustrate the difference that may be felt by a soul that has become aware of itself, as the Christ, or as Jesus the man became aware of the Spirit of the Father through those experiences of the man as he "went about doing good," and at those periods when there was received those acknowledgements of the Father that he *was* the one who could, *would*, through those activities, become the Savior of man. First, as "in whom I am well pleased;" then as "This is my son; hear ye him!"

In the overcoming, then, He *is* the way, the manner in which individuals may become aware of their souls that are in accord with that as may be one with the spirit of truth; for corruption inherits not eternal life. The Spirit is the true life. Then, as individuals become aware of that ability *in Him* to be the way, so they become the door, as representatives, as agents, as those that present the way; and the door is thus opened; and not to the man but the spirit of self that bears witness with the spirit of truth through Him that overcame the world, thus putting the world under His feet.

So we, as heirs of the kingdom, as brothers one with Him, may enjoy that privilege as He has given to those that hear His voice and put on the whole armor; that we may run the race that is set before us, looking to Him, the author, the giver of light; for in Him ye live and move and *have* their being. Do ye become rebels? Do ye find fault one with another, that are as self heirs to that kingdom? Rather be in that humbleness of spirit, that His will "be done in earth as it is in heaven." Thus do we become the children of the Father, the door to the way, and joint heirs with Him in glory.

Let thy yeas be yea, thy nays be nay. "Let others do as they may, but for me I will serve a *living* God," who has shown in man—*all* men, everywhere—that image of the Creator, in that the soul may grow in grace, in knowledge, in peace, in harmony, in understanding.

Be ye doers of the word; not hearers only. Thus ye become the door that the *way*, the Christ, the Savior, may enter in; for *he is* the way, the truth, and the light.

(Q) *As it was given in the last reading "Let none be afraid," clarify and explain the cause of fear and tell us how one seeking to awaken the soul forces may conquer same.*

(A) *Self* awareness, *selfishness*, is that that makes men afraid. The awareness of the necessities of the carnal forces in a material world seeking their gratification. Know ye not that whether ye live or die ye live or die in the Lord? As He gave, "If thine eye offend, pluck it out. If thine hand lead thee in error, cut it off."

When one has set the ideal, and knows what the ideal represents, and then knows self measured by the ideal, one sees, is aware of that lacking or that overdone in self, and plucks it out, and beholds *not* the mote that is in his brother's eye but considers rather the beam that is in his own eye.

Then, when one is set in the manners that there is fear cast aside by the wholly relying upon His promise, one may demand that to be fulfilled in that He said, "He knoweth what ye have need of before ye have asked," and he that trusteth in Him, though the heavens may fall, though the earth may pass away, His word faileth not; yet *men* act rather as if all depended upon whether tomorrow was the day of reckoning. Know ye not that he that watches lest his own feet stumble is in the way that the Father, the Son, may guide day by day? Not that ye would sit and wait for the morrow, but use that opportunity, that privilege, that birthright, that promise, *today!* Be joyous in the labor that is before thee! Be the *best* of whatever position thou doth occupy; as a wife, the best *wife* in the whole community; as a friend, the *best* friend; and there is the friend that sticketh closer than the brother; yea, the friend that gives rather his life for a friend. Ever gave ye the truths that thine brother might enjoy even a moment's rest in the Lord?

Peace be to him, peace *is* with them, contentment is in thine hand, that becomes not afraid, but trusts rather in Him.

(Q) [295]: Please give me a message on The Open Door, that I may contribute to the lesson.

(A) Learn first that lesson of cooperation. Become less and less selfish, and more and more selfless in Him. Be not afraid to be made fun of to become aware of His presence, that self may be a channel through which the glory of the Father may come unto men in a manner that all may know there is a glory, even an Israel, of the Lord.

(Q) Is there any message for the group as a whole at this time?

(A) Be patient, long–suffering, bearing one another's burdens. Be joyous in the Lord. Be not tempestuous in manner, thought, act or deed; rather *serving* in humbleness of spirit. Enjoy the labors. Enjoy those things that make for the unison of thought in Him, knowing ye have been called, and that "By *His* power I, as a member of such a group, called to give myself first, called that self may become a channel, called that I as an individual may cooperate with my brother *everywhere* in making known the joyous words of the Lord; "for the Lord is in His holy temple, let all the earth keep silent. Who *is* this Lord? Where is His temple? Know ye not that your bodies are the living temple, holy and acceptable unto Him, would ye walk in His ways?

Hark! O ye children of men! bow thine heads, ye sons of men: for the glory of the Lord is thine, will ye be faithful to the trust that is put in each of you! Know in whom ye have believed! Know that He is Lord of all, and His word faileth not to them that are faithful day by day: for I, Michael, would protect those that seek to know His face! We are through.

[GD's note: Tears, silence and beautiful attunement followed above reading. EC on waking said he had a vision during the reading, had to leave the room a while; said he saw each of us as we should be and as we are.]

Reading 2072-11

(Q) Please give advice that would help in those times when there is the beginning of Kundalini to rise or there is the circulation of Kundalini through the body. What should be the next step?

(A) Surround self with that consciousness of the Christ Spirit; this by the affirmation of "Let self be surrounded with the Christ Consciousness, and the *directions* be through those activities in the body-force itself."

Do not seek the lower influences, but the Christ Consciousness.

Text of Reading 262-46

This psychic reading given by Edgar Cayce at the Edmonds' home on Pennsylvania Ave., Norfolk, Va., this 28th day of May, 1933, requested by those present.

PRESENT

Edgar Cayce; Gertrude Cayce, Conductor; Gladys Davis, Steno. Minnie & C.A. Barrett, Esther Wynne, Florence & Edith Edmonds, Frances Y. Morrow, Hugh Lynn Cayce, Mildred Davis & Ruth LeNoir.

READING

Time of Reading 4:25 to 5:10 P.M.

GC: You will have before you the Norfolk Study Group #1, members of which are present in this room; also their work on the lesson Love. We present a copy of the preparation so far, a copy of which I hold in my hand, and seek guidance in completing this lesson. You will answer the questions that may be asked.

EC: Yes, we have the group as gathered here, as a group and as individuals; also their work and that presented on the lesson Love. Much of that is good.

Rather than presenting so many illustrations of that which may be termed as applied by seeing in others, or things, the expressions or manifestations, present more of that which may come from within.

Give as this in the experience, that each may find within self the truth, the love, the life. Life is, in all its manifestations in every animate force, creative force in action; and is the love of expression—or expressing that life; truth becoming a result of life's love expressed. For, these are but names—unless experienced in the consciousness of each soul.

Then, commune the more often in the inner shrine, in the holy of holies. Meet the presence of the Father there; *know* the love of the Christ in action; experience and see truth and the Holy Spirit in the results that come from such consecration of the ideals of self.

For, each may have the experience of speaking with Him through such a consecration; for His promises are true, "I will not leave thee comfortless, but will come and abide with thee."

In such experiences in self, then, may there be added to the lesson on Love that which will awaken in the hearts, the souls, the minds of others that desire to know *His* ways better.

Each has been chosen as a channel, and each in its own way—and not alone of self, but manifesting life through love will bring the Spirit's reaction in the daily experiences of every soul. For, they are one—*all* believe, all have heard. Then, let them that have eyes see, and ears hear, what the Spirit saith unto them in such meditation in the *inner* self.

For, from the abundance of the heart the mouth speaketh; and the love of the Father through the Son constraineth all, if each will be less selfish, less self-centered, more desirous of showing forth *His* love, His abundant mercy, His peace, His harmony, that comes from being quiet in the Lord, being joyous in service, being happy in whatsoever state ye find self; knowing that he whom the Lord loveth him doth He call into service, if each soul will but seek to know *His* way rather than "my way or thy way." Let thy yeas be yea in the Lord. Let thine understanding take hold on the things of the spirit, for they are alone eternal.

For, the children of light are called—even now—into service, that His day may be hastened, lest many faint.

Ready for questions.

(Q) *Please give a definition for, "God so loved the world as to give has only begotten son."*

(A) A beautiful lesson has just been given, and definition. This may suit those seeking this the better.

God, the Father, the first cause, seeking—in the manifestations of self—brought the world, as we (as individuals) observe it about us, into being—*through* love; giving to man, His creation, His creatures, that ability to become one with Him. That son *we* have called the Son of man, the Christ Spirit, the love made manifest in bringing the creature into material being in a plane we have called earth. That son was shown, then, the way, through the love of the Father, and He made manifest that love in giving His earthly, material life for a cause, an ensample, a mediation, a contact with the Father, a mediator for man. Hence in love, through love, God *is* love, in the Christ Consciousness, the Christ Spirit; the Son of man made same manifest in all the experiences through the earth. Hence, as given by the beloved disciple, "God so loved the world as to give His only begotten son, "that we, *through* Him, might have life—God—more abundant. He, though He were the Son, learned obedience through the things which He suffered. He that climbs up any other way than accepting those things that are to be met day by day, even as He, seeks through some other channel. The servant may never be greater than the master. He has given that we may be equal and one with Him, yet through Him, His manifestations, in Him, we live in the earth, we move and have our being.

(Q) *What is meant by the children of light, as just given?*

(A) They that choose to be guided by His will and do not, through themselves, attempt to manifest self rather than the will of the Father.

In the beginning was the word, and the word was God. He said, Let there be *light*—and there was light. Like begets like. It *is* both cause and effect, and they that choose some other way become the children of darkness; and they are these: Envying, strife, hate; and the children of these are sedition, rebellion, and the like.

The children of light first love, for "Though I may have the gift of prophecy, though I may speak in unknown tongues, though I give my body to be burned and have not the spirit of the Son of man, the Christ Consciousness, the Christ Spirit, I am nothing." For, the children of light *know* Him; He calleth each by name.

(Q) *[404] and [462]: Please give us a message in regard to our experiences.*

(A) Be ye patient in well doing. Count not the time long, for in so doing ye give the forces of doubt a place in thine own experience; and he that doubteth, or looketh back, is worse than an infidel. For, unto thee has come much, in joy, much in peace; and the little discouragements that make for faltering, if the heart will be kept singing, will make for the brighter joys, the greater appreciations, and the glories of the Son may be made the brighter in thy experience. For, live each day as if ye were to meet Him the next; in that expectancy, in that glory, and let not those things that would hinder have a place in thy consciousness. Thus do *His* children, His brethren, manifest that faith that removes mountains.

(Q) *[69]: When may I expect the promise given me to be fulfilled?*

(A) In waiting, in being overanxious, oft does one delay the appearing. Open rather thine self, and know that He will speak with thee. "Be not afraid, it is I." Then, when self is open, there will come—not one, but many—such experiences.

(Q) *How may I open self more than I am doing?*

(A) By entering more into the holy of holies, into the inner self.

(Q) *[295]: May I have a message on the lesson?*

(A) In self may there be manifested that love, even as He showed in thee, in the experiences in the ministering with and for Him; and the promises that were made thee *are* true, if self will be kept in that way in which that spirit of love, of faith, of hope, of charity, may be kept in His way. "If ye love me, keep my commandments" is ever the call of Him.

(Q) *[993]: Why do records entities are making come constantly to me, and a desire to know more about them?*

(A) As has been given thee, there were those experiences in which those that consecrated and set themselves as individual souls to accomplish definite conditions in the experiences and the affairs of the sons of men, were the records kept by self. Then, this experience of seeing, feeling—visioning, even, at times—the records made by entities, by groups, is just a portion of self's development towards those marks of higher calling as may be set only in Him. For, through the glorying in Him, and not in self, do we become conscious of that He would accomplish *through* us. So keep, even as was said of her of old, "She pondered these and kept them in her heart," knowing that there would be revealed—even as they may be put to service for others—that as each soul may need for the stimulation of *its* soul in a broader, better service in His name. For, there be no other name given under heaven whereby men be saved.

(Q) *Please explain what was meant in the Life Reading given [329] that he would be offered work on the 15th of May?*

(A) The way was opened; and ye may assist him in understanding what is to be done in the material and mental self, for the carrying on is to only give the understanding in the relationships to time, space, condition, relations, and individuals.

(Q) *Any message for the group as a whole at this time?*

(A) Take that as has been given, that ye—each soul—enter into the quietness of self and seek to know His bidding with thee at this time. For, as it has been given, there is a cause—a purpose—for which the group was called, and enjoined, that each study to show self approved unto Him, avoiding the appearances of evil, *rightly* dividing the words of truth, life, light, and love; and by thy conversations, by thy deeds day by day, make manifest that love He has given, He has shown, in the earth.

We are through.

A.R.E. PRESS

The A.R.E. Press publishes books, videos, audiotapes, CDs, and DVDs meant to improve the quality of our readers' lives—personally, professionally, and spiritually. We hope our products support your endeavors to realize your career potential, to enhance your relationships, to improve your health, and to encourage you to make the changes necessary to live a loving, joyful, and fulfilling life.

For more information or to receive a free catalog, call:

800-333-4499

Or write:

A.R.E. Press
215 67th Street
Virginia Beach, VA 23451-2061

ARE PRESS.COM

EDGAR CAYCE'S A.R.E.

What Is A.R.E.?

The Association for Research and Enlightenment, Inc., (A.R.E.®) was founded in 1931 to research and make available information on psychic development, dreams, holistic health, meditation, and life after death. As an open-membership research organization, the A.R.E. continues to study and publish such information, to initiate research, and to promote conferences, distance learning, and regional events. Edgar Cayce, the most documented psychic of our time, was the moving force in the establishment of A.R.E.

Who Was Edgar Cayce?

Edgar Cayce (1877–1945) was born on a farm near Hopkinsville, Ky. He was an average individual in most respects. Yet, throughout his life, he manifested one of the most remarkable psychic talents of all time. As a young man, he found that he was able to enter into a self-induced trance state, which enabled him to place his mind in contact with an unlimited source of information. While asleep, he could answer questions or give accurate discourses on any topic. These discourses, more than 14,000 in number, were transcribed as he spoke and are called "readings."

Given the name and location of an individual anywhere in the world, he could correctly describe a person's condition and outline a regimen of treatment. The consistent accuracy of his diagnoses and the effectiveness of the treatments he prescribed made him a medical phenomenon, and he came to be called the "father of holistic medicine."

Eventually, the scope of Cayce's readings expanded to include such subjects as world religions, philosophy, psychology, parapsychology, dreams, history, the missing years of Jesus, ancient civilizations, soul growth, psychic development, prophecy, and reincarnation.

A.R.E. Membership

People from all walks of life have discovered meaningful and life-transforming insights through membership in A.R.E. To learn more about Edgar Cayce's A.R.E. and how membership in the A.R.E. can enhance your life, visit our Web site at EdgarCayce.org, or call us toll-free at 800-333-4499.

Edgar Cayce's A.R.E.
215 67th Street
Virginia Beach, VA 23451–2061

EDGARCAYCE.ORG